BEATING THE ODDS

BEATING THE ODDS

The Rise, Fall, and Resurrection of a Sports Handicapper

BRANDON LANG

WITH STANLEY COHEN

Skyhorse Publishing
A Herman Graf Book

Skyhorse Publishing books may be purchased in bulk at special discounts for sales promotion, corporate gifts, fund raising, or educational purposes. Special editions can also be created to specifications. For details, contact the Special Sales Department, Skyhorse Publishing, 555 Eighth Avenue, Suite 903, New York, NY 10018 or info@skyhorsepublishing.com.

www.skyhorsepublishing.com

10 9 8 7 6 5 4 3 2 1

Library of Congress Cataloging-in-Publication Data

Lang, Brandon.
  Beating the odds : the rise, fall, and resurrection of a sports handicapper / Brandon Lang with Stanley Cohen.
      p. cm.
  Includes index.
  ISBN 978-1-60239-680-7
 1. Sports betting. 2. Gambling systems. 3. Gambling--United States. I. Cohen, Stanley, 1934- II. Title.
  GV717.L36 2009
  796--dc22

                                        2009028002

Printed in the United States of America

For my mother, my wife Kim, and my daughter Ireland Jade, you are and always will be the air that I breathe.

—B. L.

To Betty,
who, over a journey of more than fifty years,
has beaten the odds at every turn . . .
and taken me with her.

—S. C.

CONTENTS

Prologue   xi

CHAPTER 1:   In the Beginning   3

CHAPTER 2:   Finding My Way   17

CHAPTER 3:   Learning the Trade   33

CHAPTER 4:   The Million Dollar Man   45

CHAPTER 5:   Super Salesman   59

CHAPTER 6:   The Fundamentals of Handicapping   75

CHAPTER 7:   The Bubble Bursts   91

CHAPTER 8:   A Brief History of Sports Gambling   105

CHAPTER 9:   The Future Beckons   113

CHAPTER 10: Connecting on the Links   127

CHAPTER 11: Slouching Toward Hollywood   139

CHAPTER 12: Caddy to the Stars   151

CHAPTER 13: Skimming the Cream—Gretzky,
Jordan, Woods   169

CHAPTER 14: On Hollywood's Red Carpet   177

CHAPTER 15: Back to Basics   187

CHAPTER 16: Changing Seasons   209

Addendum: The Case for Sports Betting   225

Afterword: Looking Ahead   237

Sources   241

Acknowledgments   243

"The greatest pleasure in life is gambling and winning. The next greatest pleasure is gambling and losing."

—Nick the Greek

PROLOGUE

No one grows up with dreams of becoming a sports handicapper. It's not an occupation that you find in career catalogs or hear about at job fairs. There aren't any such listings in the want-ad sections of newspapers. I don't know of any colleges or universities that offer degrees in the subject, and there's no way to train for it. It's something you might fall into if you have an existential taste for unknown endings, nerves that are immune to sudden turns of fortune, and the twinkle-in-the-eye suspicion that luck is always tugging at your sleeve.

At the core of every sports handicapper is the soul of a mystic who feels he can divine the future. If the numbers are read correctly, if proper weight is given to nuance and form, you ought to be able to pick the winning side more often than not; provided, of course, luck does not choose the wrong time to turn its head and betray your trust. But the hazards of the trade go far beyond wins and losses, for sports handicapping is an extension of a multi-billion-dollar enterprise that is legal in only a handful of states and that, in most jurisdictions, flourishes just beyond the reach of a system that seems to embrace gambling on anything but team sports.

All the same, sports gambling is one of America's most lucrative industries. About one billion dollars a year is bet on sporting events in Las Vegas alone, and that is just a fraction of what is wagered across the country. Best estimates put the total at more than 50 billion dollars; at least 500 million is bet on the Super Bowl and twice as much on the NCAA men's basketball tournament known as March Madness. It is not possible to project an accurate figure, for most of the action takes place under cover. Neighborhood bookmakers, many of them affiliated in small consortiums, have traditionally covered most of the bets. In recent years, offshore Internet sites have been cutting themselves an increasingly generous slice of the pie. But the handle—the total amount wagered every year—continues to rise, driven largely by television's exhaustive coverage of sporting events.

There has always been an umbilical connection between sports and gambling, which is alternately denied and condemned by the leagues and the television networks that indirectly profit from it. It was fed initially by the creation

Prologue

in the 1940s of the point spread, which made football and basketball exceptionally attractive to bettors. The point spread made every game, in effect, an even-money proposition; the odds were the same whether a player bet the favorite or the underdog. But the sea change came with the advent of television coverage, first by the networks, then by a bevy of all-sports stations that follow the action twelve months a year. Premium cable and satellite packages will give a viewer every NFL game and every NBA game throughout seasons that continue to grow in length.

There would be far less demand for such outlets if it were not possible to get down a bet on a game. Viewers crave a stake in the action and are far more likely to watch a game if they have reason to favor one side or the other. Were it not for gambling, the well of television money that nourishes the economy of every major sport would begin to run dry, for gambling delivers the viewers who create the audience that attracts the sponsors who fill the coffers of the networks with the vast reservoir of funds that feed the industry of prime-time sports. Television is the medium that make it universally accessible; gambling is the fuel that drives its engine.

Betting on sporting events has little in common with other forms of gambling. Casino games—roulette, craps, blackjack, poker—require the active participation of the player; he is betting on himself. Sports gambling more closely resembles the Wall Street world of business investment. The bettor is required to consider the options, to calculate the factors that inform his selection and weigh them against those that favor the other side. He is betting on the performance of players whose actions he cannot control, trying to read the future, to forecast events and determine the outcome in advance of their unfolding.

The ingredients needed to win at sports gambling are not unlike those required for success in more conventional pursuits: a certain degree of knowledge, a great deal of patience and discipline, and a fortuitous bounty of luck. The element of luck, of course, is the variable most likely to elude one's control. No matter how congenial the odds, no matter how esoteric the information he might possess, every gambler is schooled in the knowledge that there is no such thing as a sure thing. But a first-rate handicapper can often bring a bettor just that much closer to certainty; the difference between winning and losing is often measured by a perilously narrow margin.

Like most others in my trade, I came to it through the back door. My earliest ambition was to become a professional athlete. I had lettered in baseball and basketball in high school and was hoping to earn a full-ride scholarship, but somehow I managed to escape the notice of college recruiters, for I received no such offers. At eighteen years old and with no discernible direction, I enlisted in the U.S. Navy. My three-year tour was more adventurous than I had hoped for, but when I was discharged, in 1984, I still had no focus on the future.

I settled in Long Beach, California, which seemed to be an upgrade from my hometown, Midland, Michigan, worked at odd jobs, and traveled rather aimlessly for the next three years. Then, through no doing of my own, fortune intervened. My mother, recently remarried, moved to Las Vegas with her new husband and his five children in the fall of 1987, and

Prologue

she asked me to move in with them. I didn't know it just then, but the future was knocking at my door. Las Vegas was a new world for me. With the bright lights, the sizzle and pop, the nonstop action, it appeared as though destiny had sent for me. Sports had been my refuge since I was a child, and I was eager to find a career that was connected to the games I had played and followed. It was only through sports, I thought, that I could get the charge that comes with the defining moment of winning or losing.

I had been betting on games since I was in high school; nothing too risky, mostly the football parlay cards on which you had to pick four straight winners to get back $10 on a $1 investment. Even then, I understood that I was getting 9-to-1 odds on a legitimate 15-to-1 shot. I was sure I knew what I needed to know about sports betting. I was well acquainted with the point spreads and money odds involved in most propositions, and I believed that having been an athlete, I understood the mystique of sports in a way that was foreign to those who were strictly spectators. I thought I might be able to pick winners at a better rate than most bettors, and if I was right I might be able to sell my opinions. I could carve out a career as a professional sports handicapper, an heir to the legacy of Nick the Greek.

I started out modestly. I took a job with a Nevada gaming house working "900" numbers. Callers would pay $2 for the first minute and 99 cents for each additional minute to get a handicapper's best bets. But that was just the beginning. I had embarked on the swiftest, most reckless ride of my life. Before it ended, there would be high-wire escapades—some life-threatening, others emotionally draining. I would live in upscale districts, travel in designer cars with designer women, caddy at a prestigious golf course for the likes of Bill Clinton, Jack Nicholson, Tom Cruise, Sylvester Stallone, Mark Walhberg, and Wayne Gretzky, and be the subject of a major Hollywood film starring Al Pacino and Matthew McConaughey, who played me. Now, looking back, much of what happened seems to have been inevitable.

But I know that it wasn't. Wisely or not, I made the choices each step of the way, and this is how I remember it.

BEATING THE ODDS

IN THE BEGINNING

I knew from the very start that one way or another my life would be built around sports. My two older brothers, Bryan and Bill, were both terrific athletes, so I got into playing sports at a pretty early age and found that I had some ability myself. Bill, who was six years older than me, was a superstar in baseball and football, and he was my idol. At Midland High School in Michigan, he played shortstop and batted third on the varsity baseball team and was a defensive end on the football team. He also returned punts; that's the kind of speed he had. Terry Collins, a minor league shortstop who later managed in the majors at Anaheim and Houston, was the coach's brother-in-law, and he thought Bill had big-league potential. Bill was big and had raw power; he was a Cal Ripken type. Collins used to come around in the off-season and work out with Bill, hitting him ground balls and pitching to him, and I was always there, right behind him, chasing the balls that went through. Several colleges—the University of Michigan and Michigan State among them—expressed an interest in Bill, but he never got the big-time scholarship; neither did Bryan, who also had phenomenal athletic ability, and, of course, neither did I.

Bill fell victim to drugs. Bryan fell victim to crime. It was not without cause. Our family life was a train wreck. We experienced it all—incest, rape, child molestation, drug and alcohol abuse, suicide, even attempted murder. It was amazing that I made it through relatively unscathed. I think it helped that I was the youngest of the five children. The future came too late for my brothers and my sister. My clearest memories begin when I was in the fourth grade, about nine years old. The years before that are a blur. I recall incidents here and there, but I've probably tried to block them out; that's how bad they were.

We were all born in Midland, Michigan, which, as its name suggests, is right in the middle of the state, about two hours northwest of Detroit. But I have a vague recollection of living briefly in California when I was very young and of moving back and forth between the West Coast and Midland. At some point, my father had gotten a job out there and we all moved, but if there was any domestic harmony it didn't last very long. My father was an alcoholic with a violent temper, and that was not a good combination. Before long, there was a wild flare-up between him and my mother, and I remember her packing up all us kids and taking the train back to Michigan. Some months later, my father came calling with his tail between his legs, and we all went back to California, but it didn't last.

We finally settled in Midland, which was a typical small town in America's heartland. Like many others of its type, it was a company town, virtually owned and run by Dow Chemical and Dow Corning, but its familiarity lent a feeling of stability. My mom's parents were there and so were her sister and brother and their families, and she felt at home there and somewhat protected. But it was a false sense of security. My father made no attempt to stop drinking, and he grew more volatile and more abusive. Finally, it all came to a head. My mother asked for a divorce, and that really set things off. My father said he would never agree to a divorce, and he began to make other plans. His basic strategy was simple and definitive: he would kill my mom, all the kids, and complete the job by killing himself.

Ironically, his alcoholism was partly responsible for his plot being foiled, because he was roaring drunk on the day he chose to pull it off. Other circumstances also played to our favor. His intent was to wait until late in the day, when we were all home, and then he would get the job done with a 30.06 caliber rifle. But it didn't work out that way. I had had an argument with my brother Bill, and he had left the house. It was a Friday night, and Bryan and I were watching *Sonny and Cher* on CBS, and I said, "Let's go outside and throw the football around." We went outside, leaving the house empty.

While Bryan and I were playing catch, we saw two cop cars go by, then my mom's car, followed by another cop car. I waved at my mom. I was only nine years old and I didn't sense that anything was wrong. But Bryan did. We learned that my dad had been waiting in his car, armed with the rifle, and when my mom came by our house, he fired at her from the car. My mother thought that all us kids were in the house, so instead of pulling into our driveway, she went across the street to a neighbor's yard and got out of the car. By this time, my Uncle Dave, who happened to be with my mom that day, was struggling for the rifle with my dad. My dad threw him to the ground and took aim at my mother, who was running to get to the corner of the house. My father hunted a lot and he was an excellent shot, but with the liquor running through him, he was in no condition to play marksman. He tried to shoot but the gun jammed. He quickly cleared it and fired, but the bullet hit the edge of the house as my mom turned the corner. Uncle Dave had picked himself up and with the aid of a shovel he subdued my father just as the police arrived on the scene. They put him in a patrol car and took him away. He was not a first-time offender. He had done time for grand larceny auto before he married my mother, so he was already an ex-con and that would not help him at trial. Since I had seen the whole incident, I was called as a prosecution witness to testify against my father on a charge of attempted homicide.

I remember the judge questioning me before the lawyers came into the room. He asked me if I knew the difference between true and false. I told him that false meant you're telling a lie and it wasn't right to tell a lie. The judge seemed satisfied with that answer and allowed me to take the witness stand. I recall sitting in the swivel chair turning this way and that, the chair scraping against the wooden railing and the judge holding it steady and giving me an all-day-sucker to calm me down. Although I must have been a bit edgy, I don't recall being really nervous. The situation seemed very plain to me: They were going to ask me questions and I was supposed to tell the truth. It didn't matter to me who was involved or what it was about. If what he did was wrong, it was wrong. And that's the way I approached it.

Basically, I was asked to relate what I saw from the very beginning and that's what I did. I remembered that the day before, I had seen the 30.06 and a few other guns in the trunk of my father's car and I asked him what they were for. He said, "Me, you, Bill, and Bryan are going to go out a little later, maybe tomorrow, and shoot a while, take some target practice." I thought, "Oh, cool," and the next day he disappears and things go haywire and there he is shooting at my mom with blood in his eye for the rest of us. And that's what I told the court, step-for-step, right on through the police taking him away. I still recall everyone in the courtroom smiling at me approvingly, I suppose because I seemed oblivious to the pressure. It was just natural to me to tell the truth. Even when I was very young, my mother used to tell people, "Be careful what you ask him because he'll tell you exactly what's on his mind whether you'd like it or not." So I was comfortable testifying against my father because it was just a matter of telling the truth, and at ten years old I'm not sure I really understood the gravity of what he had tried to do. In the end, my father was convicted of attempted murder and sentenced to five to fifteen years in the state penitentiary.

Our family had never been financially comfortable, but with my father in prison we were downright poor. My mom did the best she could to hold things together, but we were struggling. I had a ticket for the state lunch, and everyone knew we didn't have a lot of money. We sold our house and moved to an apartment complex on the other side of town. It was called the Forest Glen Apartments and it was a wonderful place to grow up. I had no consciousness of being poor and I didn't feel deprived because most of the people around us were no better off. There was always food in the fridge and I had clothes to wear and I never paid much attention to what kind of clothes they were.

Most important, I had my brothers and sports and I knew that eventually sports would play a big part in my future. But I needed some direction; I needed someone in my life who would fill the gap that my father had left, that he never really filled at all. Bill and Bryan had already fallen off the edge. Bill was severely abused by my father, and he never got over the psychological damage. Like my father, he became an alcoholic and he was also addicted to drugs. It was pretty much the same with Bryan. He began smoking pot in the ninth and tenth grades and graduated to stronger stuff. He had great natural ability as a baseball player but he never really gave it a chance. I got lucky. At just the right time, just the right person came into my life, and very possibly saved me from a fate similar to my brothers'.

When my father was in prison, he met Pastor Stan Anderson of the Local Assemblies of God Church, and he asked the pastor to look in on our family from time to time. One day, Pastor Anderson sent a gentleman to our house who asked if any of us wanted to go to church. I said, "Sure, I'll go." I was the only member of my family who agreed to go, and I started attending church at the Midland Assemblies of God. I was in fifth grade then, and it was there that I met the first father figure who replaced my dad. He was Pastor Stan Anderson, and he placed his hand upon my life and changed it forever. Stan had three daughters, so he kind of adopted me as a surrogate son and looked after me from fifth through ninth grades, which is such a critical time, right through adolescence. For me it was especially critical because the likelihood was that there was nothing but trouble in my DNA. My dad's father committed suicide, he shot himself in the head; his brother died of alcoholism on Skid Row in California; my dad sexually assaulted my sister; my mom's brother tried to rape her. That was my heritage; I needed help to get beyond it, and Stan Anderson showed me the way.

When I was ten years old, I accepted Jesus Christ as my personal savior. It would be years before I truly understood what the spiritualism of Christianity meant, but at the start, it provided a foundation that was essential to my growth. My principal article of faith was that I never wanted to let Pastor Stan down. Any time I had to make a decision about something I knew to be right or wrong, I would ask myself what Pastor Stan would think and let that be my guide.

It was around the same time that we moved to Forest Glen Apartments that I began to find myself, to consider various possibilities and develop the character that would later define who I was. I also met a kid there who became my best friend throughout my youth. His name was Kenny Sanders. He was a year older than me, in the sixth grade, and he was black, which made us an unusual duo in Midland, Michigan, back in the late sixties and early seventies. Midland was a town of about 35,000 people, and there were probably no more than five black families in the entire community, and they all worked for Dow.

Kenny and I had a lot in common. His father had left when he was very young, and he was being raised by his mother. He also liked to play basketball. There was a nice full-court basketball court at Forest Glen and we played together every chance we had. When we weren't playing we still hung out together. We had sleepovers at one another's homes. People called us salt and pepper or, individually, half of an Oreo cookie. Some called us Piccolo and Sayers, referring to the Chicago Bears teammates—Brian Piccolo, who was white, and Gayle Sayers, who was black—an inseparable union made famous in the film *Brian's Song*.

Kenny was a practicing Baptist, so we followed the same Christian principles, and together we were immune from peer pressure. If someone tried to entice us with drugs or anything else we knew wasn't right, we each said "no" for one another. But basketball was our common obsession. We used to play one-on-one, full court, up to one hundred baskets, best-of-seven games. That was our NBA championship. We played at least three times a week. Our dream was to be the starting backcourt on Midland High's basketball team three or four years down the road.

In the meantime, I was playing other sports too, and doing pretty well at them. I was the best twelve-year-old pitcher in my Little League. We fell just a few games short of going to Williamsport, Pennsylvania, to play for the Little League championship, now known as the Little League World Series. In the first game of the playoffs I pitched a four-hitter, struck out eleven batters, and we won, 6–1, but three games later I was beaten and that was that. I was also a pretty good hitter and played shortstop when I wasn't pitching. Here again, I benefited from my relationship with my older brothers. Before we moved to the apartments, we used to pitch a tennis ball to one another with a concrete wall as a backstop in a barn on our property. My brothers could throw much harder than I could, and

I had to be pretty quick to get my bat on the ball. So I learned to react to a pitch in a fraction of a second and I developed exceptional hand-to-eye coordination. I also played quarterback on my Pee Wee League football team, but basketball remained my number one priority.

If I was going to go big-time in any sport, I knew it would be basketball. And my model was right out there and on display with the Philadelphia 76ers—Julius Erving, known to all who followed the game as Dr. J. Erving, was the first of what we might call the postmodern basketball players, those whose athletic ability sometimes eclipsed their basketball skills. The Doctor soared through the air, made spectacular slam dunks and handled the ball as if it were no bigger than a grapefruit. He was not only good, he was spectacular and what I wanted when I was twelve years old was to be like Dr. J., in the same way that years later kids wanted to be like Michael Jordan. I even had my red hair done up in a wild Afro which was later put into corn rows by Kenny's cousin.

It was around that time that a new spiritual influence entered my life. He was Dennis Campbell, the youth pastor at my church. In all Assemblies of God churches, you have your main pastor and another—a youth pastor—who just deals with the youngsters. We used to go on retreats and to camp every summer and Dennis was fantastic. He was extremely charismatic, and his personality was so over-whelming that just about every teenager in his church tried in one way or another to emulate him; I certainly did. Dennis became another surrogate father for me, just as

Stan Anderson had. And around that time I needed all the help I could get, for my real father was about to reenter my life.

My dad served only three years in prison and was released for good behavior just about the time that I was about to start ninth grade. My mother was apprehensive about my father's return; she did not want to be anywhere near him. She had suffered considerable abuse at his hands and now she wanted to get away. She decided to move to Duluth, Georgia, because she had a friend down there and she wanted me to go with her. I was not at all eager to move. I had been looking forward to going to Midland High, where I had my whole support group. But my mother pleaded with me and, very reluctantly, I agreed to leave my cocoon, to leave behind everyone and everything I knew and go with her.

So it was in Duluth, Georgia, that I began ninth grade, a high school freshman, and I did not know a single person in the school and no one in the town either, except for my sister. I got along okay; I made the freshman football team as a starting wide receiver, but I was extremely homesick, and as it turned out I had an option. My father had moved back to Midland and was ready to take me in. We had been to visit him in prison a few times and he seemed properly remorseful, but there were still issues to be considered regarding my living with him. I was aware of the hazards, I knew what the past was like, but in the end, you know, he's still your dad. Even at his worst, he continued to work at his job; he put food on the table and we always had clothes on our backs. He was a house painter and despite his drunken binges, he never failed to show up for work; he had a tremendous work ethic.

My first priority was to get back to Midland, and in a decision that still breaks my mother's heart to this day, she let me go. Had I stayed with her, I'm not so sure things would have worked out the way they did. Once again, her sacrifice cleared the way for my dreams.

Everything I understood and cared about was in Midland and it was worth any hardships that living with my father might entail. As it turned out, it worked pretty well. There were times when he would come home drunk and I'd have to get him up, take his shoes off, and put him to bed. There were a few occasions when his drinking bouts were long enough and severe enough that I didn't want to deal with them. So I would move in with my aunt and uncle, who lived about five miles away, but it was a tough five miles. I had to take two buses to get to school or walk a considerable distance, while my father's house was just a few blocks from the school. In the long run, I think I made the right choice. I was back in my environment, ready to pick up where I had left off, eager to begin my basketball career in earnest. But there were obstacles to overcome. I was entering the school as a sophomore and it was going to be difficult to make the junior varsity at Midland because it was already loaded with talent, but I made the squad nevertheless.

As circumstance had it, my high school basketball career was less than auspicious, although Kenny and I did make the dream of being the starting backcourt come true. Tom Hursey was the varsity basketball coach, and he soon took his place along with the two pastors as a significant male influence in my life. He, along with the junior varsity coach, Chuck Trzcinski, better known as TRZ, knew I had incredible talent but that it just needed to be handled the right way. I made the varsity my junior year and my game was starting to peak. Coach Hursey sent me down to junior varsity in the middle part of the year and in my four games for TRZ I averaged 24 points and 13 rebounds, which led to Tom bringing me right back to varsity and inserting me into the starting lineup for the last four games of the regular season. With Kenny and I in the backcourt together, we went to the district finals before losing to Saginaw High, the third-best team in the state, 50–48, coming from 13 points down in the last four minutes. I scored eight points in the run, all on assists from Kenny, but it wasn't enough.

The most enduring lesson Coach Hursey taught me— one that I embraced and has served me well all through my life—was the importance of attitude as an essential ingredient in achieving success. He always preached that if other things are relatively equal, a positive attitude will always make the difference. I took that to heart and in more than one instance it worked in my favor.

2

FINDING MY WAY

In truth, my options following high school were neither plentiful nor particularly attractive. Given my druthers, I would have liked to receive a basketball scholarship to a Division I college that had a good broadcasting program. I had done some play-by-play on a local radio station when I was in high school and I was the public-address announcer for the girls' basketball program and for the local men's college basketball team, Northwood Institute, so I had a notion to pursue broadcasting and communications as a career. Coach Hursey contacted a few small schools for me where he thought I might get at least a partial scholarship, but it would not be easy pickings. My high school grades were average which put me at an academic disadvantage, and my basketball career was not nearly as distinguished as it might have been had I been able to play more freely, as TRZ allowed me to during those four games on JV. For whatever reason I never played that freely for Coach Hursey, never felt I had that freedom my senior year that I'd had earlier with TRZ. You add the fact I was playing with two very selfish seniors, and I just never found a consistent rhythm all year.

A few small colleges expressed some interest, but they didn't have any scholarships available. What they were offering was preferred walk-on status, which would give me serious consideration and a better-than-average chance of making the team. I considered the possibilities and eventually settled on Northern Michigan University, a school of about 8,500 students, located in Michigan's Upper Peninsula. They had an excellent broadcasting program and the campus was only about an eight-hour drive from Midland. So I enrolled at Northern Michigan but I never got to go there. I needed financial aid and was eligible to receive it from the federal school loan program. But before I crossed the school's threshold, the Reagan administration, which had just taken office, pulled the rug on student loans. What originally was going to cost me $900 a year jumped to $4,000 a year and I had no chance.

Now, I was back to square one, and it was not just my future that I was forced to contemplate. I had to take a hard look inside myself and I decided that I was really not ready for college. I was emotionally and psychologically unsettled. Broadcasting sounded like it might make a good career but I was still uncertain whether it was right for me. I needed to find some stability in my life; I needed a personal compass that pointed me in a direction that was well defined and of my own choosing. I also decided that the Upper Peninsula was not far enough away from Midland. I wanted to put some distance between myself and my past; I wanted to go out into the world and try to become the person I was supposed to be, which in my mind was a person famous for something. I didn't know what for at the time, but I knew I'd be famous.

If you are raised in an environment as dysfunctional as mine was and you don't find a way to disown it, it becomes a part of your life. It's like an umbrella you're under. If you stay under that umbrella you're never going to know what it's like outside, you never have a chance to find out whether you can really be different, whether you can break the mold and get out from under it. I began to realize that I had to break free, I had to get away from my father, from everyone I had known and depended on and try to find my own way. But I still didn't know how to do that, how to take the first step. As so often happens, chance would soon intervene.

My cousin Jeff was living in Tulsa, Oklahoma, and I went down there to visit him. I decided to stay a while and took a job with a telemarketing firm and then left to work in a movie theater. This was in the summer of

1981 and one of the big movies of that season was *Stripes*, an army comedy starring Bill Murray. On my breaks I used to watch the movie. I particularly liked the scene in which girls were mud wrestling and slipping and sliding all over the place, and crazy as it seems, the idea of joining the military appealed to me. It seemed like a place where you would have some time to hang out and meet girls and think about what you might want to do with the rest of your life. I told this to Jeff, and he said, "Great, let's go join the marines." I told him any branch was good with me, I just wanted to join the military. So we went down to the marines recruiting office and told them we wanted to learn to be trained killers, snipers, and the recruiter was impressed by our enthusiasm. He gave us a lot of paperwork to fill out, but by the time we got home Jeff had changed his mind. He didn't want to go into the military at all. I decided I didn't want to join the marines by myself, so I went back down to the recruiting office and returned the papers. While I was there, I talked with a navy recruiter and asked him point blank whether it's true that of the four services the navy would give me the best chance to see the world. "Absolutely," he said. I filled out the papers to enlist in the navy, but for some reason I got spooked and again decided not to follow through. It was further proof of just how uncertain I was about my future.

Jeff and I hitchhiked from Tulsa to Los Angeles and what an adventure that was. It took us a total of eight rides. We got stuck at one exit for twelve hours trying to get one ride and slept under an overpass one night, but all in all, reflecting back on the trip, it was a ton of fun.

I went on one job interview in Los Angeles, at a Big 5 sporting goods for a position as a sales rep, and after the thirty minute interview I was offered the position on the spot. It would become a common occurrence in my life, getting offered a job on the first interview. I batted 100 percent in nailing the first job interview, which was the first sign I had a personality that just couldn't be ignored.

However, I sensed I was not ready for the fast-paced life in Los Angeles at this time, and I turned down the job. Instead, I took a bus to Casper, Wyoming, to visit with my mom. She had divorced my father, remarried, and moved to Wyoming, where she worked at a Holiday Inn. I loafed around for two months, stretched out on my mother's couch, gained about twenty-five pounds, and knew that I had come to the end of the line, that if I did not do something now I might float into freefall and lose my way entirely. What I needed, I felt, was a kind of discipline imposed on me from outside that would teach me to discipline myself. I called the navy recruiting office, had them forward my papers, and this time followed through with the enlistment.

The navy introduced me to a whole new life and to aspects of myself that I had never recognized. Not long after I started boot camp in San Diego, my company commander called me into his office. "I've been looking over your personnel file," he said. "You've played a lot of sports and it appears to me that you have the makings of a leader." He asked me if I wanted to be his RCPO1. The RCPO is a recruit captain personnel officer. The RCPO1 is his assistant; it's something like being an assistant squad leader in the army or marines. Of course I accepted the offer. It made boot camp a breeze and after that it got even better. I was made class leader in the senior apprenticeship training program and that gave me first pick in duty stations. The choice of a duty station was critically important because that's where I would spend the rest of my three years in service. My first priority in making a selection was the same consideration that drew me to the navy in the first place.

"Which assignment," I asked the personnel officer, "would give me the best chance to travel and see the world?" "That's easy," he said. "If you go on the Battleship *New Jersey* you'll do a world tour." I didn't need to hear anything else. I took a week's leave, went home to see my family, and reported to the Battleship *New Jersey* in Long Beach, California.

Once aboard ship, my run of luck continued. It began to appear as if every authority figure I ran into in the navy was there strictly for my benefit, as things were breaking my way at every turn. The personnel officer on the *New Jersey*—his name was Vinny something—looked through my file and liked what he saw. He said, "You know, you don't have to serve on deck; I can put you anywhere you want to go." "Really?" I said. "We need people up on the bridge," he said, "in the navigation department, quartermasters. You plot and navigate the ship. The ship pulls into port, you're the first to get liberty. It's a lot better job than working the deck." "You sold me," I said. "I want to go to navigation."

So there I was, up on the bridge, working with officers, plotting the navigation of the ship. Even better, part of my quartermaster training involved learning how to steer the ship and I seemed to have a natural feel for it. I first learned to control its speed and then to steer it and I really felt I was in my element. There were two master helmsmen above me—second- and third-class quartermasters—and they needed a third. I took the test, passed it, and, at age nineteen, I became the youngest master helmsmen ever to steer a battleship. A year or two later, I became one of only three sailors to steer the *New Jersey* through the Panama Canal.

But for most of that first year we remained in Southern California, and it couldn't have been better. The *New Jersey* had two softball teams, the blue and the gold, and we were very competitive with one another. I was on the Blue team, and in one of the biggest tournaments on the West Coast, we beat the Gold team and faced the Navy team (coached by the All-Navy coach Mike Jones) from the base in Port Hueneme in the championship game. We lost the game but I did my best, crushing two homers and throwing out two guys at home from my position in center field. After the game, Jones came up and asked me if I wanted to get picked up to play in his next tournament. My senior chief Mike Binder, who was at the game, said it wouldn't be a problem. Two weeks later I was selected for the 1982 All-Navy softball team. What that meant was that for the next two months I did nothing but travel all over California playing softball.

When the softball season was over I segued directly to basketball. It wasn't played on as broad a scale as softball had been, but I was the starting two-guard, the shooting guard, on our ship's team. We had a pretty tough club. I was the only white guy on the team. We had a good six-foot-nine player in the low post, and two six-seven forwards. I had become twice the player I ever was in high school and was playing with unbelievable confidence. I averaged 25 points a game, and I was approached by an officer who suggested I transfer to the U.S. Naval Academy in Annapolis, play basketball for them, and become a naval officer. But that involved too long a commitment—four years at the academy and then another four years in service. I was more than satisfied with my three-year term. I was having a great time, and in June of 1983 we were preparing to leave on our world tour.

The cruise began simply enough. We started out in Hawaii, then traveled to the Philippines, Thailand, and Singapore. From there, things became a bit dicey. This was 1983 and there were problems in Central America—in Nicaragua and El Salvador. The *New Jersey* was dispatched to the area, but we were there chiefly as an intimidating presence. We parked off the coast for about a month doing nothing more than giving tours of the battleship to distinguished visitors. But our next stop, which was totally unexpected, was serious business. We thought we were headed home from Central America, but Uncle Sam had other ideas. The Middle East was heating up and we were on our way to Lebanon. Our original three-month cruise was about to become a seven-month journey. We were stationed about three miles off the coast of Beirut on October 23, 1983, when the Marine barracks at Beirut Airport were bombed and 241 servicemen were killed. President Reagan brought the marines home, but the *New Jersey* remained where it was, firing missiles into the hills of Beirut by way of retaliation. The projectiles, weighing 2,500 pounds, were fired from sixteen-inch guns in an intense barrage, sometimes in volleys that numbered in the hundreds. It was a stressful time. We knew that there were missiles capable of reaching the ship from the coast and there was no way of knowing what would happen next. All told, we were on the ship for more than four months without once setting foot on land; it would be eleven months before we returned to the States.

There was, however, some relief when we left Beirut. Our last port before going home was in France; it was a fitting reward. We had put together a basketball team on the *New Jersey* and we played the French national team in a gym up in the Alps. They had a big front line—seven foot, six-eleven, and six-nine—but their guards weren't very big and their team as a whole was slow. The refs, we learned upon walking into the gym, spoke virtually no English. I was acting as coach of our team as well as playing shooting guard, and I had an interpreter next to me when we discussed the rules. Both teams played a two-three zone and both teams could shoot from the outside. We had a three-point lead with the clock winding down, but then the refs took over the game. They made some terrible calls. It was clear that they were determined not to let us win the game. We had the ball with eleven seconds to go, holding a 93–92 lead, and were whistled for traveling. It was the third bad call in the final minute of the game and I pulled the team off the floor. We never completed the game. Nonetheless, we were given medals for participating, and there were no hard feelings. The coach of the French team apologized to me for the way the game was officiated. He gave me his card and told me to call if I wanted to play for him after I got out of the navy. In fact, my enlistment was coming to an end. I was offered shore duty in Hawaii if I re-upped for another three years, but I had had enough; I knew it was time to move on.

In August 1984, four months before I was to be discharged, I met the first love of my life, a girl named Cassie Vida. She lived in Harbor City, which is in Southern California, and I decided to settle there too. Ironically, it fulfilled an informal commitment I made to myself when I was a kid back in Midland. I was a big Michigan football fan, and I remember watching the Wolverines get beat by Southern Cal in the Rose Bowl, it seemed every New Year's Day. I used to sit there looking out the window; it was freezing outside and turning dark, and there on the TV screen I was looking at sunny California, the green grass, the bright red-and-gold Trojan uniforms, the frisky, sharp-looking cheerleaders, and saying to myself, "That's where I'm going to live," and now here I was. I rented a room from a lady who happened to be the mother of David Pack, the lead singer of the rock group Ambrosia. I was living where I had always wanted to live, dating a good-looking girl. All I needed was to figure out what I was going to do with the rest of my life.

At the time, I didn't feel a sense of urgency. I had just turned twenty-two, and I felt like I could take my time while seeking the right direction. When you get out of the service, you need to reprogram yourself to a certain extent. For the previous three years I didn't have to do much serious thinking. In the military, you're told what to do and someone else is largely responsible for the outcome. Now I had no one to rely on but myself. I still believed my final destination would be somewhere in the sports field, but I didn't know where or exactly how to find it. In the meantime, I took a job as a warehouse worker at a glass company in Long Beach. I was a foreman's assistant. My job was to assist with the cutting of the glass and then to load the glass onto trucks. The cutting was done with a $750,000 computerized cutting machine that I had been taught to operate. The foreman and I would do this all day, five days a week, and I was making pretty good money. After about six weeks, when the foreman hurt his back, I was made foreman because I was the only one who knew how to run the cutting machine. I was given a 50 percent increase in salary, but it didn't end well. One day, I got my leg caught in the cutting machine. Thinking the machine was going to go further up the table to make a cut, I had turned my back and it sucked my right leg right into it. Had I turned into the machine instead of away from it I probably would have lost the leg. But it was bad enough. I was rushed to the hospital and it took 120 stitches to close the wound. The leg healed all right, but I was determined to seek another line of work.

Not long after that, Cassie and I broke up. Without a girl, without a job, with no real connection to sports, I was beginning to feel adrift, that I was going nowhere but where the wind would take me. Once again, I felt I had to start over. This time I decided to seek professional help. I went to a big Los Angeles employment agency, and they got me a job that put me on track to what could have been a career position. I was hired by the prominent Wall Street investment banking firm Drexel Burnham Lambert where I worked directly for the fabulously wealthy, soon to be notorious, Michael Milken. I started out at entry level, working as a courier. Milken had 130 brokers working for him and he wanted every one of them on the floor every minute it was open, thinking about nothing but turning small profits into large ones. He did not want them dealing with details or distractions. So every broker had his own personal secretary and each secretary had a number of people at their disposal. So if, for instance, Mr. Ackerman called his personal secretary and said, "Listen, I want my Porsche taken to the car wash and I need my dry cleaning picked up and dropped off at my house," the secretary would call a courier to run Mr. Ackerman's errands and then, maybe, to go to his $5 million home and wait for the cable guy to arrive.

Well, here I am on Wilshire Boulevard in Beverly Hills in the employ of Michael Milken, king of the junk bonds. Every Monday morning I was handed a five-star menu from a catering service and I'd write down what I wanted for lunch each day, and from Monday through Friday I would have a gourmet lunch right at my desk. Other than that, I'd sit around, read the sports pages, and wait for my phone to ring. There were also side benefits. If I was taking Mr. Ackerman's car to the Porsche dealer, I might drive around Beverly Hills awhile looking to pick up chicks and playing Mr. Cool. If I waited at some guy's mansion for the repairman to show up, I'd hang out at the pool and raid his refrigerator. It was a wonderful job for a twenty-two-year-old guy just out of the navy trying to decide what he was all about. I would be sitting with Michael Milken in his office—he might not know me from a hole in the wall—and the next thing you know I'm doing a bank run with $2 million dollars in cash in a briefcase, flanked by two security guards.

One day, it seemed as if the future might have come calling for me. I was sitting in Milken's office and, for the first time, he appeared to take some notice of me. "You're doing a good job here," he said, "have you given any thought to your future?" I told him I wasn't sure yet about what I wanted to do, and the next thing I know he offered to pay my college tuition if I wanted to work for him as a broker. To this day I don't know why I didn't accept the offer, but something about it didn't register with me. I trusted the sixth sense that I had always counted on and politely turned it down. Just about a year later my instinct was justified. It was revealed that Drexel Burnham Lambert, and Michael Milken in particular, had been involved in illegal activities in the junk bond market. The firm was driven into bankruptcy (it went out of business in 1988) and Milken went to prison on finance-related charges.

I had left the firm just before the scandal broke. Still unsure of my future and lacking any real sense of direction, I chose to return to my roots. I went back to Midland, moved in with my aunt and uncle, and got in touch with Coach Hursey. One thing I was pretty certain of was that I wanted to get back into sports in one way or another. Hursey made me his assistant basketball coach at Midland High, and I began working with the kids in other ways as well, as what you might call an informal counselor. A number of youngsters in the high school system were identified with Down Syndrome, which is a chromosomal disorder, and I started working with them. I assisted the teacher who ran that program and felt I was making a difference, doing something constructive. For added measure, I started working as a DJ for the local radio station, doing play-by-play of high school sports. To flesh out my income, I got a part-time job as a porter at the Holiday Inn, setting up banquet tables, happy-hour buffets, and taking care of odds and ends. During the summer, when school was closed, I worked at a nearby church summer camp, sharing my Christian values with the kids while also giving them some lessons in sports.

I was having a great time; my plate was full, I was squeezing out a living and I had begun playing basketball again. I was averaging thirty points a game in a church league and, at twenty-three, I was in the best shape of my life. One Monday night in December 1986 I was playing pickup basketball at Northwood Institute, a small college in Midland, when I ran into a guy who played a pretty good game. We played H-O-R-S-E and I beat him and then I beat him playing one-on-one. He asked me if I had ever played college basketball. I said I hadn't. It turned out that he was the assistant basketball coach at Evangel College, a Christian school in Springfield, Missouri, associated with the Assemblies of God. He told me I was better than any of the guards he had in his program. He said he would like to give me a full scholarship but that none was available at the time. He suggested that I enroll in September and join the team as a walk-on. Then, he said, he would be able to give me a three-year scholarship. It sounded great to me. I put together all my financial aid papers and I was looking forward to the trip. But a few months later, in February 1987, I blew out my left knee in my church league's championship game. I tore both the meniscus, which is cartilage, and the ACL, the anterior cruciate ligament. There was no chance that I would be healed and ready to play ball in the fall.

As things developed, I had a number of other opportunities to mull over for the fall. Coach Hursey approached me at the end of the 1987 school year and told me the public school system had created a full-time position for me doing what I had been doing, working with the Down Syndrome kids and assisting Hursey with the basketball team. At the same time, I was offered a regular job as a DJ with the local AM radio station I'd been working for. For added measure, a friend called and said that Dow Chemical had a spot for me if I wanted it. It was the radio job that had the most appeal. It was a chance to get into the field that I had been interested in from the start and I snapped it up. I did some local sports and was given a program list for the music I was supposed to play, and I did whatever a radio DJ does. I worked from 6 to 10 AM on Sunday and 6 to 10 PM from Monday through Thursday. It was just what I wanted, because it left me free to continue the high school work I'd been doing on a part-time basis.

In many ways it was an ideal situation. There was just one sticking point. I was twenty-four now and I knew that if I settled in too comfortably I would spend the rest of my life in Midland, Michigan. That was not what I wanted, and by the end of the month I was gone from Midland forever. Where I was headed would turn my life in a new direction and open vistas I had never dreamed of. In November 1987 I was on my way to Las Vegas.

LEARNING THE TRADE

Nowhere could have been farther from Midland, Michigan, than Las Vegas, Nevada. No place I had been— not even Paris—could match the sense of sizzle and speed that Las Vegas conveyed at first sight. I felt that I was somehow destined to find here what I had been looking for but, still, it took a while to find out just what it was.

My mother had married a Mexican fellow by the name of Ted Isais, and he came with a family of five children— two sons and three daughters. They had a four-bedroom house, and I moved in with them. There were eight of us living together and it was the happiest time of my life. The kids were all in high school or junior high; I was their big brother. Actually, given the age difference, I was more like their uncle. My own siblings, not surprisingly, had been having their troubles. My sister, living on the East Coast, was on her third marriage. Bill was still battling drug addiction. Brian had gone to prison for robbing a restaurant, had been released, and then went back again for stealing a safe from a Wendy's while working in concert with my cousin Jeff. But things eventually evened out for Brian. Working on a prison farm while on parole, he met the woman who became his wife. Now, more than twenty years later, they are still married and living in Las Vegas with their two sons. Brian managed to turn his life around completely. He has a master's degree in social work and operates his own agency that works with children who have disabilities in foster care.

Though still unsettled, I was happy as a pup living with my mom, Ted, and my five new siblings. I had taken a job working for an appliance company, driving around Vegas, delivering washers, dryers, and TVs to people who rented them by the month. One day, on the car radio, I heard a commercial that set me on my course. It was for a national broadcasting school, one of those 800-number ads you hear all the time: "You want to be a DJ? Then come to National Broadcasters and start a career in radio or television. Call our 800 number. . ." I called the number, enrolled in the school and, though I didn't know it quite yet, I was on my way.

Learning the Trade

I kept my job with the appliance company, which financed my tuition at the school. I had also started betting on sporting events (this was Vegas, wasn't it?) and I was doing rather well. I recalled that when I was in high school I used to play those parlay cards that seemed to make their way around every high school in the country. You had to pick four football games against the point spread and if you hit them all you got back ten times your investment. I would put down $2, and more often than chance would allow I got back $20. Of course the people who financed the parlay cards were doing just fine. The true odds against winning four straight games are 15-to-1. They were giving what they called 10-to-1, which was really 9-to-1 because two of the dollars I got back in the twenty were the same two dollars I had laid out when making my bet. Nonetheless, I was moving gradually into a mode that would soon become my lifestyle. I was practicing broadcasting and handicapping sporting events.

I was also playing basketball again. I joined a health club called the Las Vegas Sporting House. It was the most popular health club in Vegas, open twenty-four hours a day, seven days a week, and it was a haven for college and NBA players who were in town to gamble and wanted to work out and play some basketball during the off-season. When they could put ten players together, they had a full-court game. If they needed a few to fill in, they would choose from among the available talent at hand, guys who were not of their class but who knew their way around the court. I was often picked up as the eighth, ninth, or tenth man, which meant I got to play with Jordan, Magic, some of the best players in the country. Of course I couldn't handle them one-on-one, but playing against the other add-ons I more than held my own. This was the summer of 1988. I was twenty-five years old and back in perfect shape; my knee felt great. I was even picked by a team to play in the Sporting House Winter League.

I was at the broadcasting school just a few months when the instructor suggested that I make a tape of my voice for the Nevada Sports Schedule. The Nevada Sports Schedule served many functions. This was in the days before the Internet, before cable sports stations ran current scores of games in a crawl at the bottom of your TV screen. Nevada Sports Schedule had the local Vegas scorephone number which bettors could call for scores of games while they were playing golf or at a show. It also had one of the nation's first 800 toll-free score phones, which updated scores of games every five minutes. It printed a sports schedule that had the official Nevada rotation—a number next to the team you wanted to bet that matched the number at the sports book. The Nevada Sports Schedule was also one of the first operations to get into the 900-number industry in the late eighties.

The instructor at the broadcasting school thought I had the right voice for radio and he knew I had a betting interest in sports. He saw me call the local sports phone often enough and come back to class all excited that I had hit another three-team parlay. So he told me to make a tape and to see a guy named John Winstrom. "They're looking for score-phone announcers," he said. "You'll be perfect. You understand the games, you understand gambling, you love sports, and you've got a great voice." Winstrom listened to my tape, called me into his office, and said, "You have the best voice of anyone I have working here. I don't have a place open right now, but I'm going to hire you anyway because I don't want to lose you." He spot-used me for about a month before I got a regular position.

The main 800 number was a straightforward score phone. You'd call that number and get an update on the latest scores. But the local newspaper carried an ad for a number at which Nevada Sports Schedule offered what they called their premier pick of the day. The pick was free but before you got it you'd hear a promotion for one of their 900 numbers. Jim Feist, the owner of Sports Schedule, was also their chief handicapper. He had the local score phone for gamblers and a nationwide score phone that sold its picks as well. When you called the 800 number for an update, you might hear a recorded voice tell you that Jim Feist has a big play for you today, and the hope was that you would call Feist's 900 number, where you paid by the minute, so while the premier pick was free, it might cost you a few bucks before you got off the phone.

During my first month there, my job was strictly routine. These were the days, just a few years before the Internet obliterated all competition, when the audio text industry—the 800 and 900 numbers that provided instant information—was exploding. Jim Feist had a 900 number from soap alert, where he dished the latest news on soap opera personalities; he also had basketball superstars and baseball superstars, and those tapes were running constantly. My job was to sit in a room and every twenty minutes I'd flip the soap alert tape so it could run the other side. I'd set my little egg timer, then go over to the sports room and watch the games on TV. When my egg timer went off I'd run back in there, turn the tape, and reset it. But the industry was growing at an incredible pace and they only had one guy working the 900 numbers. So John Winstrom told me he'd like me to work there two days a week.

Soon, a score phone shift opened up and I worked three days a week at that. On the score phone side, I would just sit in front of the TV set and do a scoring update every five minutes. But I learned that it was the guy working the score phone who made the free premier pick of the day. I started making the picks on the days I was working the score phone, and I opened with a phenomenal streak. I hit something like fifteen of my first sixteen picks. It was great. I was offering my opinion to the public and it would only be a matter of time before word spread that Brandon Lang has an opinion and a damn good one at that.

On the 900 side, there were four distinct handicapping numbers—the Jim Feist Sports Hotline, Larry Ness and his Private Play, the Chip Chirimbes A Play, and Gary Austin's Executive Play. The calls cost $2 for the first minute and $1 for each additional minute. A caller would be held on the line for at least forty-five seconds of analysis before going on to a pick, and the idea was to keep him on the line as long as possible to build up the cost of the call. I was doing production work on all the lines. They loved the way I worked in the promos, and I was paying close attention and learning every aspect of handicapping a game. I learned about shifting point spreads, about the difference between public line moves and smart-money moves, the importance of weighing the intangibles that most folks aren't even aware of. I soaked it all up and when my time came I was ready.

Early in 1989, when I had been with the Sports Schedule for about a year and a half, Jim Feist came to me and said they planned to drop the Gary Austin hotline but that they wanted me to keep it going for the next fifteen days. So I took over Gary's line and, in a way, I revolutionized the industry by adding a new dimension. I implemented a system called cross-plugging. Here's how it worked:

Let's say you called Larry Ness's 900 number. You would hear Larry's voice, "This is Larry Ness . . . you've reached my private plays, charge for calls is two dollars first minute, one dollar a minute after that . . ." and then he'd go into his analysis, eating up about forty-five seconds before giving his first play. After he gave his first premier pick, I would cut in: "Before we get to Larry's next play, you've got to go to Gary Austin's hotline right now. Gary has his NBA game of the year, a play he has never lost. Call Gary today; he won't let you down; he's going to hit his game of the year for the eleventh straight year." All of Larry's calls were cross-plugged to Gary Austin. I did the same with Chip Chirimbes's number and with Jim Feist's as well. So no matter which of the other numbers you called, you ended up with Gary Austin, which was my line. I hit the NBA game of the year and another featured play the next day. Over the last two weeks in February I went twelve of fourteen on Gary Austin's number. Not surprisingly, his number made more money over that period than the other three combined.

I was well established now as the number one guy at Sports Schedule. I was their best announcer and their best handicapper. I was working on the score phone and the 900 lines. I was the only one who could do both. We were all being paid the same hourly rate and it seemed reasonable to me that I deserved more money. I took my case to Jim Feist. He looked me straight in the eye and said, "I'm not going to restructure my pay scale to suit you." "Fine," I said. With that, I knew that we would soon be parting ways.

During this time, I was playing regularly in the Sporting House's 1988 Winter League. I was in great shape, averaging thirty-six points a game and having the time of my life. One Saturday morning, I was playing in a pickup game, guarded by an older guy. He was pretty good but I was hot and having a big day. After the game we sat down and started talking. It turned out that he was Keith Starr, an assistant basketball coach at UNLV, the University of Nevada at Las Vegas. He asked me if I had ever played college basketball. I said I hadn't and gave him a brief summary of my athletic history from Northern Michigan University to Evangel College. I told him that

I had blown out my knee and that it took me more than a year to fully recover but that now the knee felt great. "I'm in the best shape of my life," I said, "and playing better than I ever had." "I think you can help us," he said. "You might be just right for our program. We need some kids who can walk on and play a little and also get good grades." I thought that last part was pretty funny.

I had just turned twenty-six, and if life had taught me anything during those years it was to be a realist. I knew there was no chance that I could walk on at UNLV and be a starting player or even come off the bench for significant minutes. But I thought I could be a tremendous practice player. Strong varsity teams need solid players to scrimmage against, players who can force them to play tough defense and make them work for their shots. Starr thought I should give it a try; he offered to introduce me to UNLV's head coach, Jerry Tarkanian. I went to Tark's restaurant; Keith met me at the door and introduced us. Tark said, "I hear you can play." "Yeah," I said, "not bad for a white boy."

"I'll tell you what," Tark said, "we have a preconditioning program that starts when school starts, in September, and lasts for two months. If you can make it through and show me you're serious, I'll let you walk on."

"That's all I can ask for," I said. We shook hands and Keith said he'd be in touch.

I won the scoring title in the Winter League and was looking forward to trying my luck at UNLV, but it didn't happen. Playing pickup on a Sunday morning, I planted hard going baseline on the left side and hyperextended my left knee. I tore the meniscus and it sidetracked me for two months. September was drawing near and I had a critical decision to make. On the one hand, I could spend the rest of the summer getting my knee back in playing shape and try putting it through Tarkanian's preconditioning program. As an alternative, I was considering a job offer that could turn out to be the chance of a lifetime. I had always put my trust in what I can only call an inner voice that has served as my guide. It's something that I felt had watched out for me my whole life and it was always right on target. There was nothing spooky about it; it was not as if I actually heard voices. It was more like an instinct, a sixth sense that helped me formulate my thoughts and cut from fantasy to reality. Whatever it was, it left me without any doubt that the dream of playing college basketball just wasn't going to happen. This was the third time that something had gotten in the way of such an opportunity, and I decided it was time to let it go.

The job offer had come about two months after Feist had turned down my request for a raise. The proprietor of one of the largest, most profitable sports betting establishments in the country—we'll call him Walter Abrams out of respect for his privacy—was in the market for new talent. He was based in Farmingdale, Long Island, about thirty-five miles east of New York City. He had just been given four 900 numbers and he didn't know what to do with them. Looking for help, Abrams called Dennis Paulson, the head of advertising for the Nevada Sports Schedule, and asked him who was the best handicapper and telephone personality he had. Paulson didn't hesitate to name me. He said, "If you want to take one guy away from Jim Feist, Brandon Lang is your man."

Walt called and we hit it off immediately. He hired me, hijacking me away from Jim Feist. But at the outset I was not working exclusively for Walt. He had hooked up with Ty Gaston, who ran a smaller sports phone company in California. I started working for Walt, in conjunction with Ty, and it wasn't long before I saw there was something wrong with the arrangement between them. Gaston was also connected with a handicapper by the name of Mike Warren, who was one of the biggest operators in the business, and they were charging Walt $50,000 a month to advertise on Mike Warren's network, which included publications as well as phone lines. Walt was calling me every day, giving me the ad copy he wanted run on the score phone, and it didn't take long for me to fall in love with his personality. He was funny, bursting with energy, and he seemed genuine; a very real guy. I told him that Gaston and Warren were ripping him off and that he should not send them the next month's payment. Walt said he was going out to California in two weeks to attend The Who's twenty-fifth anniversary concert at the L.A. Coliseum and he wanted me to go with him. After the concert, we went back to his hotel to discuss our situation. I told him that if he didn't send the fifty grand to Gaston and Warren, their phone operation would collapse, which eventually it did. He agreed not to send the payment and he asked me to come and work for him full-time. The next thing I know, I'm on a plane headed for New York.

4

THE MILLION DOLLAR MAN

If Las Vegas was the sizzle, New York was the steak. I had been impressed by the texture of other cities before, particularly by the graceful beauty of Paris, but none of them had the impact of New York. New York conveyed, simultaneously, a sense of style and power that had no equal. Perhaps most important, it pulsed with possibilities that I was sure could not be found anywhere else. It was a feeling I had even before I set foot on the ground. As my plane passed over Manhattan, I looked down over the skyline and the entire landscape seemed to vibrate with the promise of a future that defied calculation. The welcome I received and the events that followed would fulfill my every expectation.

When I entered the terminal at JFK Airport, my duffel bag slung over my shoulder, I saw a uniformed chauffeur holding a sign that read "B. Lang." It felt great seeing my name held up by a limo driver; I had always wondered what it would feel like to be met that way at the airport. Even the tiring flight on the red eye could not diminish my enthusiasm. The chauffeur introduced himself and said he was Walter's driver. He led me to a limousine that was equipped with a television set, juices, Danish pastries, and a fully stocked bar. We crossed the Throgs Neck Bridge into the Borough of Queens and headed east to Farmingdale, Long Island. We pulled up in front of a two-story building right off Hempstead Turnpike and behind a gas station. The upper level housed the salesmen, the secretaries, and the inner workings of the 800 number service. On the second floor there was a pool table, a fully equipped gym with a treadmill that faced a projection screen and four smaller TVs so you could watch all the games. There was also a security guard you had to get by to get into the room. I had a desk that was in front of the TV screens and I watched films of the previous week's action, game after game. As you headed to the rear of the downstairs level, there was a room with a Jacuzzi, bath and a shower, and Walter's office which was a room that could have been located in the NASA Space Center. There were telephones everywhere and a wall filled with TV screens, each tuned to a different channel. But the benignly bizarre character of the room was not as distinctive as its occupant.

Two years older than me, Walt was a short, round man who resembled a penguin and moved like one. He was a compulsive gambler and an even more compulsive eater. He would balloon up to two hundred fifty pounds, then take off as much as a hundred pounds, go back up to two-twenty, then down to one-ninety. When he decided to lose weight, he attended meetings of Overeaters Anonymous, an organization I had never heard of until I met Walter. Years later, in a movie called *Two for the Money*, Al Pacino portrayed him as a manic compulsive who did everything to excess but who also was engaging, witty, and possessed a folksy kind of wisdom that at times could be incredibly perceptive. And that's how he was. Though he never met Walter, Pacino had the man nailed to a tee. In the movie Pacino spoke in double time, with very little pause, as if taking a breath might break his chain of thought. That was Walter.

He offered me a seat and proceeded to look me over as closely as a breeder might examine a racehorse he was hoping to put to stud. Finally, he squeezed my arm and said, "Whoa, look at you; the Marlboro Man. Jesus, you're in great shape."

"I've been in better," I said.

"Modesty's not a virtue," he responded. "It's a vice, as evil as vanity. You'll find there are rules to success, and rule number one is know what you know and know what you don't know. Rule number two is I need to know everything you know as soon as you know it, if not sooner. Did you ever sell anything?" he asked, and then without waiting for an answer, "If you can sell, you'll never starve."

He followed his own advice scrupulously. If Walter's lips were moving, which was almost always, he was selling something to someone or someone to someone else. Right now, he was selling himself to me. He pressed a button and the TVs on the wall filled with the previous Sunday's football games. Then he explained—not that I needed the explanation—the relevance of Sunday's games to Monday Night Football.

"Do you know why Monday Night's the most watched game of the week?" he asked. "Because Monday's the last chance bettors have to recover what they lost on Sunday. If they happened to win on Sunday, it gives them a chance to go for the kill with house money. Sports betting is illegal in forty-six states, including this one; but what we do is 100 percent legal. We're performing exactly the same function as a stock broker, except that instead of touting stocks we're advising people on how to bet. We make the big money off our client list. When a client makes money following our advice, he's more than willing to pay to get our picks."

Finally, like any good salesman, he moved to close the deal. He asked me how much I was making in Vegas and said it was chump change. He told me to write down the amount that I thought I should be paid, looked at it, and tossed it in the wastepaper basket. Then he said, "I'll pay you fifty-two thousand a year," which was considerably more than the number I had written. "I'll also pick up the tab for your rent and utilities and pay for tickets for any concerts or sporting events you want to go to during your first year in New York. Do we have a deal?"

You bet we had a deal.

Walt gave me the four 900 numbers he had received from a gentleman by the name of Jerry McCarn in Atlanta. McCarn had a stranglehold on the 800 score phone business on the East Coast and he was active in other parts of the country as well. He was a major presence in forty to fifty cities. The deal was that McCarn gave Walt the four 900 numbers and Walt would pay McCarn to advertise his sports service on all of his 800 numbers. If you called one of McCarn's 800 numbers from anywhere in the country, the first thirty-five seconds would be recorded advertisements. If you were a gambler waiting to get the scores of games, you'd first hear that Walt Abrams has his game of the year. That's where Walt would get his leads, from the score phones. In the eighties and early nineties, before the advent of the Internet, these recorded numbers were huge. The number of leads that came in was unbelievable. So Walt gave me the four 900 numbers and told me to make them work.

"Starting now," he said, "you have a new identity. You're Mike Anthony, the Million Dollar Man. You do just what you did in Vegas. You make your picks and record them every day; once a day Monday to Friday and five times a day on the weekend. Each call is worth twenty bucks a shot. Right now, we're getting a few dozen hits a week.

We should be doing triple that. The first time you hit a winning streak, the phone will be ringing off the hook. Gamblers can smell a winner. What you have to remember is that you're selling the world's rarest commodity—you're offering certainty in an uncertain world."

"You want certainty?" I said. "You want those 900 numbers to boom? Give me one ad on the 800 score phone; twenty seconds. Give it to me on Tuesday night—one ad, one time, and I'll make these 900 numbers work."

Tuesday was prime time. Traditionally, a gambler's week ended on Sunday night. On Monday he would settle up with his bookie. But Monday Night Football pushed the schedule back a day. Now, on Tuesday morning, the new betting lines would be available and bettors would begin their own handicapping of the week's games. That was why I asked Walt for the Tuesday night slot. But he was reluctant. I think he didn't want it to appear that he was giving the new kid on the block an edge over the guys who had been working for him for years. Finally, during the second week of the NBA season, he came to me and said, "Okay, you can have the Tuesday score phone, but you're going to have to earn it. I want you to promote the first ever Mike Anthony Million-Dollar Three-Team parlay. I'm giving you three NBA games; you've got to nail them all." Fortunately, I loved all three games. I had twenty seconds to make my pitch, and I went on saying:

"Hey, everyone, it's Mike Anthony, the Million Dollar Man with the Billion Dollar Plan. Tonight, for the first time ever, I'm

offering my million-dollar, three-team NBA parlay of the year to the general public. It's won ten years in a row and it will not lose tonight. It pays six-to-one and it's all yours on Mike Anthony's 900 number: 900-360-3100."

The phones lit up. It was going to be a big money night. The first game was easy. The Knicks were a four-point favorite over the Nets and they won by ten. The next two were tougher. Detroit, getting eight against Atlanta, lost by seven and barely covered. The final game, from the West Coast, made me sweat. The Lakers, minus nine at home against Golden State, trailed by ten at the half. But they tied the score at the end of the third quarter, took the lead in the fourth, and beat the spread by one point with six seconds left in the game.

In addition to hitting the three-team parlay, I used the same cross-plugging technique I used in Vegas to send callers to the lines of both Tony Montana and J. C. Lagratta. On Lagratta's line I offered his underdog play of the year, which won, and Montana's double-digit special—the Sonics over the Clippers—came in by about twenty points. I was five-for-five; nearly 450 calls came in that day, 379 of them to Mike Anthony. With the calls going for $20 a pop, the total take was about $9,000 for the day. That was just the beginning. Most of the callers who hit that parlay stayed with me for the next two and a half years. It was a big score and I was beginning to attract some attention in the boiler room, which was the name we gave to the room in the office where all the action took place.

The following Monday, I was talking with Walter when his top pro football handicapper came in. He appeared not to notice me, and looking straight at Walter, he said, "The Miami-Jet point spread jumped a half tick to ten."

"What do you think?" Walter asked him.

"Miami's still a lock; I'm keeping it on my sheet."

Walter turned to me and said, "Jerry's our top handicapper. He came to me right out of grad school. Jerry, meet the new kid in town."

"Whoa," Jerry said, "phone guy makes good. Big jump from the 900 numbers. Watch out you don't get a nose bleed. I have to get back to work."

"Pleasure meeting you," I said. "By the way, Jerry, New York's gonna win straight up. They always play the Dolphins tight. Tonight, they win outright."

"Really?" Jerry said. "You have to work your way up to the NFL here, Sonny."

And that's what I did. The Jets won the game straight up and I went twelve for fourteen with the pros on Sunday after going twenty for twenty-four with the colleges on Saturday. I continued to stay hot. Night after night, college or pro, I kept on winning—two for three on most nights. If I had a losing night, I'd come back with a bigger play the next night and hit it.

The money was pouring in now. Of course Walt didn't get it all. The proceeds went directly to a company called Telesphere, which paid the revenue on the 900 numbers. Telesphere would hold back a percentage for charge-backs and taxes, and Walt got paid from the balance. The total was substantial; he was making millions and the entire operation was ready to escalate. Picking winners was just a part of the process; you also had to be a salesman. The real money was in getting high-end bettors to pay you in advance for your selections. That way, you collected, win or lose. Usually, the big players had won with you before, so if you lost the game they would probably go with you again. If the game came in as a win, you were on your way to mining gold.

Walt had a direct 800 service number which was answered by a secretary. She would say Walt was on another line and tell the caller that if he left his number Walt would call back. She also would ask, "How much do you bet on a game?" Walt never called back unless the caller was a "whale," someone who bet $25,000 a game or higher. Otherwise the number was turned over to one of the salesman. If the guy said he was a dime bettor—$1,000 a game—the salesman would call back and say, "Walt's on another call right now; I can give you his underdog shocker absolutely free, just as we advertised. But let me tell you something. Walt's got a game going tonight that he has inside information on. Basically, the referee is in his back pocket and he can practically give him the final score before the game is played. But the pick is going to cost you five hundred dollars. I can't give it to you for less. It cost Walt a ton to get the information. He has to charge for it accordingly."

What you have to do now is get a player who is accustomed to betting $1,000 a game to increase his bet substantially, because if he's paying you $500 for the pick, he's putting up another $100 with his bookie in vigorish. (All wagers on sports events require the bettor to add 10 percent to his bet. That is the bookie's commission, known in the industry as the vigorish, or the juice. If a dime player wins his bet he gets $1,000; if he loses it costs him the $1,000 plus the $100 in vigorish.) So if you do the arithmetic, he would be risking $1,600—$500 to you, $100 to the bookie, plus the $1,000 bet—against the possibility of a net profit of $500 if his pick comes in. If the guy takes the bait and sends you the money and the game comes in, you have him, he's hooked. If the game loses, you tell him, "Look, the ref guaranteed the game and he's dead meat now. But I've got an even bigger play for you tonight and I'll give it to you at a bargain price." The entire concept was based on making big bettors out of small ones; that took salesmanship and I was as good at selling as I was at handicapping.

If a $500 bettor was turned over to me, I would call him and say, "I know you're basically a five hundred dollar player, but I have a special game tonight and I'll need at least that much to give it to you. You'll have to move five thousand on this game. Will your bookie move five thousand dollars? When I get this kind of information we have to hammer it hard. Can your bookie cover five thousand? If he can, have Western Union wire me five hundred and call me back for the pick." Five minutes after Western Union delivers the money he calls and I tell him, "Okay, put five large [$5,000; actually he will have to put up $5,500, including the vig] on the Knicks minus six and a half. Enjoy the win and I'll talk to you tomorrow."

I know for certain that I'll talk to him tomorrow. If he loses, he'll call to complain that I got him in over his head with a bad play. If he wins, he'll probably call to send some of his winnings back in. If he doesn't call, I'll call him. He's a $500 bettor who just won $5,000 probably for the first time in his life. When he hears my voice on the other end of the phone, he thinks he's listening to the voice of God.

"How're you doing, buddy?," I'll say. "Hey, I apologize for last night. I said the Knicks would cover by twenty and they only covered by fifteen. Listen, I have another game going tonight. Get used to it because this is what I do; I make you money. I make your dreams come true. What you need to do now is wire me a thousand dollars." If he balks at that, I'll say "Bill, who made five grand for you last night? Let me explain something to you. You sent me five hundred last night; you send me a thousand today, that's fifteen hundred. You won five thousand last night, so if my arithmetic is correct you're up thirty-five hundred since you called me yesterday. Get the picture? You shoot me over a thousand now, then you call your bookie and move ten thousand on the game I'll give you." If you hit that game for him it's over, you own him. Before long, he'll be giving you $5,000 and betting $25,000 on a game. Basically, gamblers are chasing a dream. It's not just the money. They're looking to game the system, to get a purchase on the future, and they're ready to pay you to help them do it.

That first year I couldn't lose for winning. I hit well over 60 percent of my picks, which is incredible. My clients were making money, Walter was making it faster than he could count it, and I wasn't doing too poorly either. At the end of the year, Walter called me into his office and handed me a bonus check for $31,000. He sent me to Hawaii for a brief vacation, and when I came back there was a Porsche 928 S4 sitting in my driveway. There was no question that by now I was the main event. The other handicappers, who were all there before me, weren't happy about it, but I was too naïve to notice and Walter simply didn't care.

"I have three guys who can handicap and twenty who can sell," he told me one day, "but I only have one who can do both."

"You mean me?" I asked.

"No," he said, "I mean Mike Anthony." And he was not making a casual distinction. Walter had a new plan. He wanted me on TV, up front and visible, he said. "Big bettors want to feel they have a personal relationship with the guy they're entrusting their money to," he told me. "They want to know more than the sound of his voice, they want to know what he looks like. You're not just an adviser to a gambler; you're his ally, his advocate, and you have to let him know it. 'I don't want your money,' you tell him; 'I want your bookie's money.' You're with him all the way, and he'll trust you with anything; he'll trust you with his wife, fully naked."

It was not just a matter of making sound picks now. I was going to be transformed. Walter was intent on creating a new person. "It's not a part," he told me, "you can't act it or play it. You have to live it; you have to *be* Mike Anthony. That's the only way it will work; you have to sell it all the way. As of now, Brandon Lang is as dead as Kelsey's nuts. He doesn't exist anymore; Mike Anthony has taken his place."

My pitch did not leave much room for improvement. It had been working just fine. But my physical appearance was given a complete makeover. I was supposed to be Mike Anthony, the Million Dollar Man, and it was necessary for me to look and act like a millionaire. I was redone from top to bottom. I was given a new, slick hairstyle. I was put on a diet and a workout schedule to make me look more fit. I was tanned to a shade that suggested both health and a leisure style that befits a man of means. I always came on dressed in a suit, shirt, and tie, and they were custom made and impeccably chosen. I drove a Porsche. Everything about me was fine-tuned, and I loved it, at least for the first few years. Even today, there are characteristics of my dress and style that owe something to Mike Anthony. My suits are tailored and I take care to see that I am always carefully groomed. I also carry myself a bit differently; I'm more polished and much more at ease in public. I owe that to the years I spent as Mike Anthony.

Walter said he intended to build an empire around me, and for a brief time he did. When the TV show opened, in 1990, I was primed and ready. With great anticipation, I listened to the countdown: "five, four, three, two, one, and . . ." looking straight into the camera that had its light on, I was off and running:

"Mike Anthony here, the Million Dollar Man with the billion dollar plan. From Wall Street to Tokyo to Hollywood, all your big money stays and plays with me . . ."

5

SUPER SALESMAN

The television persona was a perfect fit for Mike Anthony. I came on each week with a new spiel, a swelling roar of bravado: "The Million Dollar Man sounds kind of small to me. Maybe if you change the 'M' in million to a 'B' I could get behind it. All you can do is win with me and there's no limit to how much. The key to victory is anticipation—the ability to see the future and react to it, and that is what I do." I was beginning to believe my own fabrications. My ego was growing larger and it was being fed by an uncanny run of success. My winning percentage defied all the odds of probability, and it continued week after week, from season to season. And if something more than statistics was needed to affirm my mystique, I got it from Walter. "I got the next Jimmy the Greek here," he would say. "Nostradamus was a novelty act compared to this guy."

Gradually, it dawned on me that my relationship with Walter was somewhat off-center; he was beginning to see himself through me. He looked at me and saw something he had always wanted to be, but couldn't. He saw a six-foot-three, reasonably good-looking, athletic figure who had a flair for self-promotion and what appeared to be an eerie intuition of future events. Walter was five-four and the exact opposite of what an athlete might be expected to look like. He treated me like a rock star and tried to get me to act like one, because if he could not be a rock star himself, he would be able to do the next best thing— he could attach himself to one. You don't always see how dysfunctional someone is when you first meet them. You need to peel away all the layers of illusion before you get to the center of their personality. Walter's problem was that he wanted to be me and in creating Mike Anthony he was fashioning the person he wanted to become.

In the meantime, I began developing some of my own clients. I didn't work in the boiler room with the other handicappers. I had my own office and went about things in my own way. There was a lot of resentment because I was the new kid on the block and I had been ordained the star. But I got along with the other guys as well as could be expected, and they were a source for some of my leads. I never stole any of the names, but I would pick up some of the prospects they were unable to hold. I would just go into the boiler room and say to one of the salesman, "Hey, give me a name, give me somebody you haven't been able to keep happy and let me have some fun." I never asked for a big-bet player, someone who would move twenty, thirty, or forty thousand dollars on a game. I always asked for a one- or two-hundred-dollar bettor. I didn't take whales; I used to take small fry and turn them into whales.

That was the high for me, taking a fifty-dollar bettor who had been doing nothing but losing and making him a winner. I would look for a guy who bets fifty dollars a game and run his bankroll up to ten thousand dollars. Then I would put him on a plane and send him out to Vegas, get him a room and arrange for a couple of hookers to be sent up and I would know that I created a new image for this guy. I helped him fulfill his dream. These were my own clients. I kept their action completely separate from what I was doing with Walter and he never knew anything about it. What I did behind closed doors stayed behind those doors. Ironically, Walt would not have approved of the way I worked with my clients. He taught us to get as much money up front as possible and to make them pay to get your picks. That way they understood that you were selling them something that had a specific value; you got nothing for nothing. I didn't work that way. I liked to win a little for my clients before I hit them up for money because if I charged them right away and lost a few, they were going to be pissed at me and I'd lose their action. So I always wanted to work clients off to the side on my own because I knew that if they got a few free winners they'd be inclined to stay with me when they dropped one or two.

A prime illustration of this technique was the owner of a dry cleaners by the name of Amir. I met Amir by chance one night at Mickey Mantle's restaurant in Midtown Manhattan. We were both sitting at the bar and watching the Knicks–Jazz game on television. It was just the first quarter but he was sweating it out; I knew immediately that he had something riding on the game. The Knicks were losing early and he was agonizing over every play.

Finally, I said to him, "Hey, buddy, the Knicks are laying seven and a half, it's the first quarter and you're driving me nuts here. Relax. You want to get upset, get upset in the fourth quarter." But he kept on squirming and groaning. "Look," I said, "you're ruining my dinner. You keep this up and one of two things is going to happen— I'm going to knock you out or you're going to leave the restaurant. Now calm down. You want to scream at the TV, do it in the fourth quarter when there's five minutes to go, you're laying seven and a half and you're down ten. That's when you have a problem. Right now, we're only halfway through the first period. Who do you have in the game?"

"The Knicks," he said.

"I have the Knicks too," I told him. "I have the Knicks minus seven and a half, and relax, it's going to be okay. The Jazz are playing their fourth game in five nights. They look fresh for the first half, maybe for three quarters, but in the fourth quarter the Knicks are going to clamp down defensively; they're going to go on a run and they'll win the game by ten. So relax. Bartender, give this man a drink."

Amir looks at me and asks, "What do you do?"

"What do you mean, what do I do? I do exactly what I just showed you; I advise gamblers on the outcome of sporting events. So enjoy your drink and watch the Knicks win by ten." The Knicks won by twelve, if I remember correctly. When the game was over I said, "Give me your number, man, I'm going to make you a personal specialty case of mine. Give me your number and I'll make you rich."

The next day I call him up and say, "Are you ready for this? Here we go." I give him three games that night and hit two of them. I think he bet $500 on each game, so he picks up $450. I call him the next day and have him bet $1,000 on one game and he wins. The next day, I give him two games. He bets $2,000 on each and hits them both. So now he's up almost six thousand. I call him and say, "How're you doin'? You're feeling good, aren't you? Of course you're feeling good. You've never won like this in your entire life. I know you haven't because I can tell guys like you. Do me a favor. You need to make me feel good now. You want some more of this action? Shoot me down two thousand dollars." And he never hesitated. Why would he? He just made more money in less time than he ever had in his life, and he got it all free. I hadn't made a nickel so far. But I would now. Amir sent me money regularly and he stayed with me until the very end, which, as things played out, would not be to his advantage.

Of course I was lucky with Amir. I hit five of our first six bets, so even if I had been taking money up front he would have stayed along for the ride. But giving him those first six games free was enough to make him a believer. He continued to pay in advance for my picks and we both did very well for quite a long time. Walter never knew about Amir or any other clients that I picked up on the side. I handled them differently from the way I dealt with Walter's clients. But in both cases, the same skills were necessary for success: I had to be able to handicap games and of equal importance I had to know how to sell. The sales factor was a constant. As a handicapper, you sometimes miss plays and have a bad run every now and then, but if you can sell you can make a client believe that your losing streaks were somehow beyond your control and, in fact, that a new winning streak is just around the corner. And I was nothing if not a salesman. You give me someone's ear for five hours and I'll have him running down the street naked singing "Kumbaya."

The pitch on a game is very important. Bettors rarely have a strong opinion unless they have an emotional investment in one team or the other. Fans have their own psychology. But most games are a puzzle to average bettors because they haven't followed the teams closely, they don't have access to the essential stats, and they can make an equal argument for either team. They like playing the home team, but the price looks a little too high.

Super Salesman

Players who are uncertain about a game usually prefer the underdog because they feel they are getting a head start in a contest that could go either way. When they call for your picks they are hoping you can clarify the situation by giving them the information they don't have but need in order to make an informed decision. So you have to be absolutely positive and offer every possible assurance. And you have to come at them like a tidal wave, fast and overwhelming, like I did in this pitch for a Dallas Cowboys–New York Giants game:

> *Dallas is 9–1 in their last ten ATS [against the spread] coming off a divisional home game. I gotta tell you something—Dallas is going to win this ball game and they'll win it by double digits. New York comes into this game 1–7 ATS after playing Philadelphia. They don't show up after playing Philly. Philly seems to drain them for some reason. Also, indoors or on turf they're 0–9 ATS in their last nine. So every stat I have supports Dallas in this game. Get all over Dallas. They'll win it by two touchdowns and you'll be ready to roll.*

It's not hard to be persuasive because those who are calling are already at least halfway persuaded. They trust you because you're a professional and you know more than they do. It's the same as if they ask the opinion of their lawyer or accountant. When they come to you they have already crowned you an expert; you're a professional,

65

you're making a living selling your advice. They want to follow that advice. It offers a sense of security they need but don't have. If they had been winning on their own, they wouldn't be calling you in the first place. Their making the phone call is a cry for help.

In this business, you have to assume that every person who calls you is a loser. That's one thing Walter taught me. Your prospective client calls and you say: "Jimmy, how you doin', babe? Mike Anthony here. You just saw me on TV? You like that tie? It's a five hundred dollar tie; not my Sunday tie. Before we do anything else, I want you to do one thing. Set the phone down, go in the bathroom and wash the 'L' off your forehead because you are a loser. Now put the phone down and go wash the 'L' off your forehead."

"Then," Walter told me, "you unplug the phone." I said, "What are you talking about?" He said, "If you leave the phone dead for a while and he's still there when you go back and pick it up, you've won him for the rest of your life." It's amazing. It works because you're selling a dream. You can win for him more than he can win on his own. When you win, that feeling you get is the greatest feeling in the world. He starts at $100 a game and he keeps going higher. The stunning thing about this industry, this business, is that the more a gambler wins, the more he has to win. The stakes keep growing and he has more money to move and he keeps going until the bubble bursts. And the bubble *always* bursts.

The inveterate bettor, the compulsive gambler, is always chasing something he can never finally reach. It's like trying to reach the horizon. No matter how far you move toward it, it continues to recede. By definition, you can't reach it. It's the same story with a gambler who's chasing a dream. Walter had a theory, and I think it's mostly correct, that many high-stakes gamblers are subconsciously playing to lose. It's a human instinct to go as close to the edge of the abyss as possible without falling in. A gambler feels most alive when he is on the brink of losing it all. One more touchdown for the other side and everything goes with it, down into the void. Even when he wins, he's still looking for that thrill, the possibility of losing everything, of teetering at the very edge of the abyss and yet finding a way to step back and save himself. It's a feeling that offers a hint of triumph, of ultimate survival. It's all going down the drain, you've just created for yourself the worst possible nightmare and yet you realize, "I'm still here, I'm still breathing, I'm still alive." In order to really live you have to be aware of your own mortality, and losing a bet that seems beyond recovery is one of the best ways of doing that. When you win, you defy death. But when you lose, you survive it, and that is remarkable. You have been there and back, and so you know what death feels like but you have escaped its embrace. The big-time gambler has the need to keep reminding himself that he is still alive, he needs to feel something, to convince himself that he still exists; he needs to put his finger on something that's really *real.* That's what keeps him going and that is what kept me and Walter going.

Of course there are many bettors, probably a large majority, who remain in control. They know their limits and stay within them. They're the equivalent of social drinkers who enjoy their pre-dinner martini or a glass or two of wine but never become hooked. I handled a great many of that type of bettor—$50 a game, maybe $100 here and there—and if they had a good run they might go as high as $500 or a dime. But they didn't chase the dream; when they began to lose they would most likely pull back rather that up the ante. They had their own psychology of betting and their own methods of finding ways to lose. The biggest mistake a general sports bettor makes is that he bets with his heart instead of his head. When you begin from there, you've already lost any objectivity in picking games. And objectivity is what you have to have when you begin to handicap a game. You have to start from scratch. The lines come out and you know what they are, but if you have a disposition to lean one way or the other you've already begun to influence how you see the game because you're going to be handicapping it from the point of view of the team you favor. If you're a Lakers fan, you're viewing the game from the Lakers' perspective even if Boston is the better bet. It's the biggest mistake that social bettors make—they let their partisan feelings determine how they bet.

The second biggest mistake is letting the previous game's result dictate which side you pick. When you approach a Sunday pro football card, you begin by writing down what you think the point spreads should be on each game. Then, you look at what the official spreads are, and you have to be careful of any game in which there is a big difference between the two. There should never be more than a point or a point and a half difference if you are on the same page with the pros who are setting the line. Why do you have a team favored by two when the linemakers are giving six and a half? Worse yet, why do you have the wrong side favored? If you're being objective, the likely explanation is that you are each handicapping the game differently. The average bettor looks at the previous week's results and maybe the week before.

Let's say Green Bay destroyed the Bears the previous week and won even bigger against the Vikings the week before that. Now they're playing a mediocre Eagles team at Philadelphia and they're favored by only two and a half, and that looks like an underlay (a game in which the favorite is not favored by enough points) to you, so you lay the points. But the previous two games may not have been true indications of Green Bay's strength and weakness because Green Bay is primarily a passing team and neither the Bears nor the Vikings are particularly strong against the pass. The Eagles, on the other hand, may have only a .500 record, but they have an airtight pass defense and they're very tough at home. The key to handicapping a game is how the two teams match up against one another. With rare situational exception—like divisional trends—if you let the previous week's game be your guide, you are betting on the wrong matchup. The chief cause of upsets is that the matchups change from week to week and very often the wrong team is favored because it has the better record and is likely to be the more popular pick. Handicapping is part art and part science, but before you begin your calculations, you have to know what to look for and you have to appraise both teams in an emotionally detached manner.

I came very close to violating my most basic rule when I was making my pick in the 2007 Super Bowl between the Colts and the Bears. It would be an emotion-packed game for me, one way or the other, because I had a 14–0–2 streak going in the Super Bowl, and as the run continued I grew increasingly nervous. The game was a big one for me and for my subscribers, but it was difficult for me to remain neutral. The Bears had been killing me all year. When I picked against them, their erratic quarterback, Rex Grossman, would have a big game and beat me. If I went back to them the following week, he would throw three interceptions and beat me again. The average bettor's impulse is to punish a team that beats him by betting against it and to reward a team that wins for him by continuing to ride it. It's emotionally satisfying but it's bad business, and I found myself caught in that very trap.

My reverse fortunes with the Bears during the regular season had already leaked into the postseason. In their first playoff game, laying eight and a half points, I thought they would blow Seattle out. Instead, they won by a field goal and very nearly lost the game outright. In the

Super Salesman

NFC championship game I went the other way. I picked an underdog Saints team to win the game outright. But the Bears won easily and buried me again. So they had me 0–2 in the playoffs, and I was 2–14 with them during the regular season. And now, here they were, staring me dead in the eye in the Super Bowl and I was beginning to feel the pressure. Their presence in the game appeared to be a personal affront. The gambling gods were out to punish me. Whether I went with them or against them, the Bears were going to beat me. They had the knife in my gut all season and now they were going to twist it.

I handicapped the game as objectively as I could. Right from the outset, I figured the Colts would be a seven-point favorite, so when the line opened at seven I knew I was in tune with Vegas. I always begin handicapping a game by asking myself which is the right side. Then, I spend a good deal of time making the best case I can for the other team. For this game, I also had to guard against letting my personal feelings get in the way. The big difference here was the quarterback advantage. Peyton Manning was without doubt one of the best ever, and he was going up against a kid I thought would work himself out of a job within the next two years. Then I asked myself if the Bears could have won their two playoff games without the home field. I didn't think so. Playing most of their home games in frigid Chicago temperatures offers an exceptional home-field advantage.

The Bears' only edge was on defense, and even that was questionable. As the teams matched up, the Colts' offense would be the Bears' worst nightmare. A no-huddle passing team, Indy would be able to exploit Chicago's chief weakness—their pass defense. They had been shielded all year by a fierce pass rush, and the Colts protected Manning like the Secret Service protects the president. Given time to pass, he would shred Chicago's overrated secondary. On the other side of the ball, it was supposed to be easy to run on the Colts, and indeed many teams seemed to run on them at will during the regular season. But in the play-offs, Indianapolis head coach Tony Dungy had put eight men in the box, up close to the line of scrimmage, and dared the quarterback to beat him. In the AFC championship game, Tom Brady, a former MVP and three-time Super Bowl champion, couldn't do it. What chance would Rex Grossman have?

Still, there was that nagging doubt, an emotional uncertainty that bordered on superstition. In every game there are circumstances that cannot be handicapped. You cannot foresee penalties and turnovers. They can beat you even if you've picked the right side. So I was concerned about that. I was also concerned about special teams. The Bears had a kick returner by the name of Devin Hester who could nullify an opposition touchdown on the ensuing kickoff. But there was no way you could pick against the Colts. They had the better quarterback, the better offense, the better coach, and a flat-out better team. I gave the game to my subscribers the night before with a predicted final score of 31–13. Intellectually, I felt as confident as you could be about any matchup. But psychologically, the pressure was more than I could handle. My Super Bowl winning streak and a slice of my reputation was on the line, and if it had to come to an end I did not want it to be at the hands of Rex Grossman and the Chicago Bears.

I had always been a ritualist when it came to watching the Super Bowl. I would sit in my house by myself, with my dogs in my lap, and watch the game with nobody distracting me. But this year was different. My nerves were stretched thin, and I could not bear to watch the game. So I decided to go to the movies, where I could find total distraction. As it turned out, I was spared a great deal of grief because the game was not a minute old before one of my worst fears came to pass. Devin Hester returned the opening kickoff for a touchdown and the Bears jumped ahead 7–0. In fact, I learned later that the Bears led 14–6 at the end of the first quarter. It would have seemed like a nightmare unfolding before me had I been watching the game. But instead it was a pair of movies I was watching, and by the time I returned home the game was about three hours old. My mom, my sister, and my six-year-old nephew, who was wearing a Peyton Manning jersey, were watching the game at my house. I was an emotional wreck when I walked through the door. My heart was in my throat. I was never more nervous about anything in my life. When I turned the corner into the living room I saw my mom smiling.

"It looks good," she said.

"It's not over yet? How many is Indy winning by?" I asked.

"Twelve."

"How much time's left?"

"A minute, thirty."

"Who has the ball?"

"The Bears."

I felt the blood drain from my head. A twelve-point lead, giving seven, with my gambling experience my first thought was "backdoor cover." That what it's called when a team that has no realistic chance of winning scores a late, meaningless touchdown that brings the final score under the point spread. My mind ran back to the Philly–New England Super Bowl a few years earlier when I actually needed a backdoor cover to keep the streak alive. The Eagles were a four and a half-point underdog and trailed by ten with less than five minutes to play. They converted three straight third downs to keep their final drive alive, and then McNabb hit Greg Lewis for a thirty-yard touchdown with 1:46 remaining and I had my backdoor cover.

I think of that now and ask my mom:

"What yard line?"

"Their own twenty," she says.

I feel the pressure ease. I'm watching as Grossman throws incomplete on fourth down to end the game. The final score is 29–17, not far from my prediction of 31–13. I had finally conquered the Bears. The monkey was off my back and the streak stayed alive. It took just a moment for all of that to sink in; then, all at once, the dam broke. I was overwhelmed by emotion and for the next five minutes tears of joy rolled down my cheeks.

6

THE FUNDAMENTALS OF HANDICAPPING

To be a successful handicapper, you've got to be able to see something that no one else sees, a hidden detail that doesn't appear in the small print and which is not to be found in any tables or statistics. You might, for example, notice that a team tires late in the game. There can be a variety of explanations: the team isn't deep enough in replacements; they haven't been conditioned properly, particularly if it's early in the season; they're a dome team or a cold weather team and they're playing in the Florida heat. You can look at that game from every angle, and if there's not much to choose from between the teams, you might figure that the game will be decided in the fourth quarter on the basis of which team holds up better.

In the gambling business, there are some things you can never account for. Again, you can't handicap penalties, turnovers, or coaching stupidity, and a lot of the time that's what beats you. So you look for details that others might not see. But while an unseen factor might finally decide which side you play, you have to begin with the traditional techniques of handicapping. As with any other line of work, there are fundamentals that must be observed when it comes to handicapping sports events. I said before that the first thing I look for is a bad line, one where there is a significant difference between what I think it ought to be and the line posted on the Vegas board. You find this most often in college basketball. Teams from smaller, lesser-known conferences can be exceptional bargains because oddsmakers can't be on top of every game. These teams—like Murray State, Southern Illinois, George Mason—frequently draw national attention in the NCAA tournament when they upset a highly seeded favorite, but you can find plays like that all through the season if you track the games closely.

You don't find bargains like that in professional sports and very rarely in college football, where powerhouse teams are rarely matched with teams from small conferences. The thing to watch for in football is the movement of the line. Because football teams play only once a week, the betting line, or point spread, is adjusted day to day.

Bookmakers move the line up or down to try to get equal money bet on both sides of the game. They don't take a position. They take their profit from the 10 percent vigorish, or juice, paid by the losers. But you have to be careful to distinguish between "smart money" moves and "public money" moves. A smart-money move is one caused by the "wise guys" in Vegas, those with big money who can swoop in right after the opening lines are posted and plunk down enough cash to move the spread. They can easily bump the line one to two and a half points in either direction if they think the oddsmakers were mistaken. A good example of a smart-money move was the 2005 Thanksgiving Day game between Atlanta and Detroit. Playing on the road, the Falcons were favored by four in the opening line, but it quickly jumped to six and then to six and a half. That's a huge move and it told me that Atlanta was the play. They won the game, 27–7.

Public-money moves are gradual; the line is moved incrementally. For example, it was public money that moved the 2005 Seattle–Carolina NFC title game in the wrong direction. The spread opened at Seattle minus six, but the media kept hyping Carolina after the Panthers destroyed the Giants and beat the Bears in their two previous road playoff games. As a result, the line dropped to four and a half. The public bought the hype, ignoring Carolina's injury woes and the fact that they had beaten two teams with suspect passing attacks. Seattle beat Carolina, 34–14. When the public moves the line, it's wise to go the other way.

"Tough beats"—games you had every right to think you had won but you ended up losing—are another trap for the average bettor. Your team has a game in hand and the spread covered, then goes into a prevent defense and gives the other team a backdoor cover. You're looking to get even by betting against them the following week, but it's almost always a mistake. You have to forget the highs and lows in this business and put your emotions aside. And you should very rarely bet on the team you root for, because it's almost impossible to be objective. A handicapper can never afford to be a fan.

It's also a given that different sports require different approaches. Each sport has its own indicators, things you look for beneath the stats. In professional football, you have to take it one game at a time. If a team loses a game it should win one Sunday, it may have very little bearing on what it does the following week. The team regroups, the matchups are different; sometimes the loss is the result of an emotional letdown following a big win, or the team might have been looking ahead to a critical game with a tough opponent the following week. Now it comes back on an emotional high, and you went the other way based on one bad game. In college football, the emotional factor is even greater and the point spreads are larger. Playing overpriced favorites is a common practice in college football where blowouts are not unusual and teams often win by thirty or forty points.

The NBA is another matter entirely. Teams play three or four times a week, making fatigue a significant factor, and linemakers sometimes overlook its importance. I'll often find teams playing three games in four nights or even four in five nights. Other elements add to fatigue: A team coming off a game in the high altitude of Denver will often have dead legs the following night, and so will teams traveling from one coast to the other with short turnaround time. My job as a handicapper is to spot these situations and evaluate whether the oddsmakers have adjusted the line accordingly.

The game that serves as the ideal model for the handicapping trade is the Super Bowl. More often than not, you have the two best teams going against one another; you have eighteen or nineteen games to study strengths, weaknesses, and trends; and you have two full weeks to make your calculations. That accounts, at least in part, for my 16-0-2 record. I begin handicapping the Super Bowl just as I do a regular season game—I watch the point spread, which requires a bit more study when there is a two-week window for line moves.

The Giants–New England 2008 Super Bowl was a particularly interesting one to handicap. New England, after all, was only the second team in history to go through the regular season undefeated and then win two playoff games. The Giants were about as long a shot as you can get in a Super Bowl. They were just 10–6 on the season and somewhat erratic. Their quarterback, Eli Manning, blew hot and cold. But as the season closed, there were signs of new life. The Giants ended the season with a remarkably good showing at home against the same New England team they were to meet in the Super Bowl. They led by twelve points before being edged, 38–35. The 35 points were the most the Patriots had allowed all season. So there was much to consider.

The Patriots were favored by twelve in the opening line, and I thought the spread was too big for a game being played on a neutral field with two weeks to prepare. Historically, one of two things happens in the Super Bowl: the favorite wins by a huge margin or the underdog keeps things close, with a good chance to win the game outright. So I began by asking myself whether the Patriots were likely to blow the Giants out; if I thought they could I was going to lay the points.

Two things had to happen for the game to be a blowout—Tom Brady would have to have lots of time to pass and Eli Manning would have to turn the ball over. So I decided that I would watch the film of the first meeting and see how the Giants put the pressure on Brady. He put up 38 points on them and passed for 400 yards. Did they put pressure on him or did he have all day to throw? The fact was that he didn't have all day to throw; he got hit all night long. He had a big play to Randy Moss; the Patriots made some other big plays and they benefited from some pretty good field position. But the Giants did apply the pressure; they repeatedly moved the pocket. I said to myself, you know what? With two weeks for the Giants to prepare, Brady's not going to have all day to throw. And we've seen over the years that any of the great quarterbacks in NFL history—Joe Montana, John Elway,

Brett Favre—they are all mere mortals if they spend all game dealing with pressure. I concluded that the first requirement for a blowout would not be met—Brady was not going to have time to throw.

Then I checked to see how often the Giants turned the ball over, and I found that in their three previous playoff games, all on the road and against some of the best defenses in the game—Tampa Bay, Dallas, and Green Bay—the Giants had turned the ball over only once, a fumble following an interception against the Packers. If Manning was able to protect the ball in near-zero temperatures in Green Bay, what would make you think that he would turn it over on a warm day in Arizona? During the regular season he was intercepted frequently and fumbled the ball more often than you would expect. What made the difference?

Kevin Gilbride, the offensive coordinator, made the difference. He had scaled back the game plan. He started putting Eli in better positions to succeed. He shortened the passing game. And it seemed to work. After the Tampa Bay game, linebacker Barrett Ruud of the Buccaneers commented on Eli's performance: "If it was third-and-eight, he got nine; if it was third-and-six, he got seven." In the NFL, shorter is often better. When the quarterback takes a three-step drop, he's looking for a curl or a slant, possibly to the tight end, on a six-yard pattern. That's a lot easier to focus on than taking a five-step drop and looking for something to clear fifteen yards down the field. By the time the quarterback gets back and plants his feet, he's got pressure coming his way and he's got to start moving around the pocket and doing some things that make him uncomfortable.

What makes a great quarterback in the NFL is time to throw. If a quarterback is afforded time in the pocket, for the most part, he's going to be successful. You can guard guys downfield for just so long before they break free. So-called experts on television and radio were calling Tom Brady the greatest quarterback of all time; if he's the greatest quarterback, it's because he has a great offensive line that has given him time to throw. Brady sat for two years at the University of Michigan and then split time with Drew Henson as a junior before finally becoming the Wolverines' starter his senior season. And if another Drew, Drew Bledsoe, had run out of bounds instead of turning up field and taking a hit that ended his season back in 2001, we might never have heard of Tom Brady. It's possible that Bledsoe might still be the starting quarterback for the New England Patriots.

Those were the basic factors that I took into account during the first week of handicapping. In the second week, I watched the film of the regular-season game between the teams six or seven times, and I came to the conclusion that New England could not blow out the Giants, not with the Giants' coaching staff having that much time to prepare. I also concluded that Eli was not going to turn the ball over, because he was so in sync with his offensive coordinator. Once I locked onto those conclusions, taking the Giants plus the points became the logical play. Was I still nervous about releasing it? Sure, why wouldn't I be? I was looking at a team that was 18–0, that was averaging more than thirty points a game. On the other hand, their record in the playoffs was not reassuring. They had struggled with both Jacksonville and San Diego at home. But it was not possible to escape the hype entirely. Everyone has a desire to believe in invincibility; we look for perfection in an imperfect world. But the fundamentals of handicapping made the Giants the play, and I released it with some confidence. For two weeks on radio and television I said I wouldn't be surprised to see the G-men shock the world and win the whole game which, as the world watched, they did.

In any game, regardless of the sport, there is a right side and a wrong side for a bettor. The right side doesn't always win, but what makes it the right side is that every principle of sound handicapping points in that direction. Of course things happen that you can't foresee—a player gets injured or has a particularly bad game; a journeyman comes off the bench and becomes an all-star for one game; the officials have a bad day. In Super Bowl XL, some poor officiating saved my streak. Pittsburgh was a four-point favorite over Seattle and I picked the Steelers to cover. As it turned out, the Seahawks outplayed them for most of the game, but some very bad calls turned the tide in the Steelers' favor and they covered, 21–10. Seattle lost but they were the right side in that game; they should have won it outright.

Handicapping a series is generally more difficult than handicapping a single game, for there are too many variables that must be considered during the course of four to seven games. For example, I had picked the Los Angeles Lakers over the Boston Celtics in the 2008 NBA finals. The West was by far the stronger conference, and the Lakers had totally dominated their rivals in the early rounds. They defeated Denver, Utah, and San Antonio, losing only three games on their way to the finals. The Celtics, by contrast, had struggled. Both Atlanta and Cleveland had taken them to seven games and they were not able to win a single game on the road until finally taking two games at Detroit. So it seemed that the Lakers had had an easier time in a tougher conference, but I was wrong. As it turned out, the Celtics were the better team, and fortunately for my clients I learned that early enough for them to get some of their money back by betting Boston in the individual games.

The Celtics won the first two games at home, which was no surprise, and then lost the third at L.A. although they covered the spread. Form was holding. But the fourth game defined the series for me. Playing at home, the Lakers blew a twenty-point lead in the third quarter and, watching the game, I saw that they didn't match up well with the Celtics. The Celtics were a much better defensive team and they had imposed their will on the Lakers, erased a huge deficit on the road, and come back to win the game by six points. They lost the fifth game by five points, but covered again, and now, going back to Boston, I was sure the Celtics were the right side, giving only four points. There was no way you could bet the Lakers. In that situation, you make up your mind to either lose with Boston or stay away from the game. I gave it to my subscribers as a way to retrieve what they lost betting the series. The Celts won by thirty-nine points and closed out the series. Boston covered every game. The Lakers were true to form. Going back to 2004 when they lost to Detroit, they were 0–11 against the spread in their last two NBA finals.

Of all the sports, baseball is the easiest one to win money at because there's no point spread; all you have to do is pick the winner. A run line is available but it is rarely quoted and only used when the price on a game is very high. You never want to bet a baseball favorite of minus 160 or more (risking $160 to win $100). If you're going to bet that big a favorite, you're better off laying the run line, which means your team has to win by at least two runs. That reduces your risk to minus 110 (the normal 10 percent vigorish). There are some standard plays in baseball that are a good investment. For example, it's very hard to sweep a team on the road, so if a visiting team has won the first two games of a three-game series, betting the home team to avert a sweep is usually a smart play.

Baseball is a game of streaks, and if you catch a team on either a winning or losing streak, you can make some money very quickly. In 1988, the Baltimore Orioles lost twenty-one straight games to open the season. If you jumped on that streak after four or five games and bet incrementally more after each loss by the Orioles—let's say increasing your wager by fifty percent—you would have made out pretty well, even though you would have been laying odds on every game.

Not unlike trading stock, you have to look for commodities that are overvalued or undervalued. Famous pitchers are often overvalued in the odds, especially if they have passed their peak. A few years ago, Randy Johnson lost three of his first four starts and he was a heavy favorite in each game. Early in 2008, Arizona's Brandon Webb started the season with nine straight wins. When he was going for his tenth, I had a free pick betting against him on my Web site. The theory was that since he was not going to go undefeated, the odds were that he would lose a game fairly soon. Denny McLain is the last pitcher to win thirty games in a season, and that was in 1968, more than forty years ago. You know it's not going to happen again, not the way pitchers are coddled in today's game. For added value, Webb was a favorite every time he started. On the day he got beat he was on the road, pitching against the Marlins in Florida, and his team, the Diamondbacks, were a 160 favorite. He lost that game and he lost his next start before coming back and winning two in a row.

Another thing to watch for in baseball is pitchers who always seem to pitch well against certain teams and, by contrast, pitchers who just can't seem to beat particular teams. One pitcher, who is a sure Hall of Famer, gave me a really offbeat explanation why he had so much trouble with the Montreal Expos. We were playing two-on-two basketball in Vegas and I asked him how often major league ballplayers got paid. He told me it was up to the player.

You can get paid every two weeks, once a month, or you can take your whole salary in one lump sum. He said you had to be careful if you were paid periodically because if your payment period fell when you were playing in Canada you would have to pay Canadian income tax since that's where you were getting paid. Then, with Canada the subject, he offered me this bit of information. The best strip clubs in any major league city were in Montreal. So, he said, if I'm ever pitching up there you might want to bet against me because the chances are I didn't get much sleep the night before. I checked his record and found he was 2–11 in Montreal.

One ingredient of sports gambling that is often over-looked is money management. If you wager the same amount on every bet, the odds say that you will end up losing because you're laying odds—usually the 10 percent vigorish—every time you wager. Many players tend to increase the size of their bets when they're losing, on the false notion that the odds have turned in their favor. They haven't. Just because you've lost three in a row, you haven't earned the right to win your next bet. It's still a single game and the teams don't know that you're entitled to have it your way. I always advise my clients to cut back when luck is running against them. But they rarely do. The high that comes with winning is an addiction; it's stronger than drugs. The feeling of being a winner is euphoric and once you experience it at the highest level you'll want to chase it forever. You should always be looking to play with house money. You bet more when you're ahead, when you're on a roll, but you should always hold some of your winnings aside because whatever roll you're on will end sooner or later.

It's here that the losers' psyche leaves its mark. While a gambler gets his highest high from winning, he is more comfortable when he is losing because that's the feeling he's more accustomed to. It also eases the pressure on him. There's a certain urgency that comes with success; the gambler begins to expect things from himself that he knows he can't continue to deliver. Losing restores a kind of order; things seem more normal. It also affords the gambler the opportunity to feel a little sorry for himself and to place the blame elsewhere: the players are choking, the coach is stupid, the officials probably have a wager on the other side. Then, after taking a drubbing because of circumstances beyond his control, the gambler now, heroically, turns it around, overcoming all obstacles and asserting his claim to a superiority of intellect and will that is proven by the numbers. He has endured and triumphed. That sense of conquest against the odds is a universal feeling among sports bettors, but it accounts for nothing.

The one certain thing about gambling is that no matter how shrewdly you handicap, luck will have its say, and the one certain thing about luck is that it changes. The fact that winning and losing so often comes in streaks is an enigma and no one has the answer. It can more easily be accounted for in the performance of athletes. A batter develops the slightest hitch in his swing and he is a tad late getting to the pitch. A basketball shooter's stroke is off by just so much and the shot clangs off the front rim. Once the defects are corrected, they're back in the groove. But there is no comparable explanation for the streaks that affect a handicapper. If you're going to make a living handicapping games every day, you're going to have winning streaks and you're going to have losing streaks. Sometimes those losing streaks are going to be really bad and there's not a thing you can do about it.

7

THE BUBBLE BURSTS

On a football weekend early in the 1993 season I went 13–1, accounting for more than $2 million in winnings. I asked Walter for a pay raise, thinking that all that was needed was for us to negotiate a figure. It never occurred to me that he would turn me down, but he did. He said let's wait until June and we'll talk about it then. June was the end of the NBA season, and that's when I got my annual bonus. I didn't think I should have to wait nine months to get what I had clearly earned. I told Walter I wanted the salary increase right then. September was the unofficial start of our season. Our major action was in football and basketball, and I was off to a very good start. It was a head-to-head collision, and Walter held firm. He had won a victory he would soon regret.

I embarked on an unofficial rebellion. Like the Velvet Revolution, it was not direct combat, just a little here and a little there, an unannounced defiance of Walter's authority. I started coming in late, taking time off; I set my own hours and it was driving Walt crazy. On the one hand, he could not bear having his authority challenged; on the other, he was afraid of losing me. I had placed Water between a rock and a hard place and was beginning to call my own shots. I came in late one Tuesday morning and found Walter sitting in my office.

"Do you know what time it is?" he asked.

I looked at my watch, but before I could answer, he said, "It's time to press. When you're winning, you press."

While he was talking, I took a set of golf clubs out of the closet.

"What are you doing?" he said.

"I have a ten-thirty tee time at Bethpage Black golf course," I told him.

"Stop screwing around," he said, "you've got a lot to do before this weekend."

I said, "I'm not asking you if I can go, Walter, I'm telling you. That's how it is, understand? You want my picks? Hell, I'll make them now."

"It's only Tuesday," he said, "you have all week."

"I don't need it," I said.

"We're going to be giving picks in the neighborhood of twenty million dollars this week."

"Nice neighborhood," I said.

"You're really going to make your picks now? No study, no analysis? Just like that?"

"Just like that," I said. "I'm in a zone, Walter. Locked in. You want my picks, I might as well make them right now."

My Tuesday picks went 3–11 on Sunday. On Monday morning, Walter was furious.

"How do you go 3–11?" he snapped. "Wanna know how? You make Sunday's picks on Tuesday, that's how. It rained in the Midwest. Two starting quarterbacks didn't play. You're a handicapper, not a psychic."

"There's still Monday night and the parlay," I told him.

"Fuck Monday night," he said. "You fucked with me, right? You were pissed because of the raise, right? Okay, we're on shaky ground here. I'll give you a bump up now. It won't have anything to do with your bonus in June. Now, what about tonight's game? Everyone's going to be looking to climb out of the hole you put them in yesterday. How strong a pick is this?"

"I love the game, Walter," I told him.

But I blew it; both the game and the over/under. And that was the beginning of the end. Some time later that week I decided to call my mother. I hadn't spoken with her for quite a while, and I suppose I was looking for some assurance, a bit of comfort.

"Brandon, is that you?" she said.

"It's me, Mom. Did you get the money I sent you?"

"I did, but it's too much, Brandon. Where did you get it?"

"I earned it," I said, "every fucking cent."

"What kind of talk is that?" she said.

I said, "I'm sorry, Mom. I was just in my Mike Anthony mode."

"Who's Mike Anthony?"

"It's a character I play on TV; that's how I earn the money."

We spoke for a while, and then she said, "You've changed, you know. You sound quite a bit different, Brandon."

And I knew she was right. I'd become a slick talker in the role of Mike Anthony, and I couldn't turn it off even when I was speaking to my mother. I was morphing into the character I was playing. I had become more materialistic. I felt that I had to flash money and the things it bought to show people that I had arrived. I went back to Vegas for a brief visit and I rented a BMW and drove to my old neighborhood to see the guys and they were shocked. I was in a fantasy football league and just for the fun of it I bid $100 for a player. Prior to that, the biggest bid ever in our league was $10. Yes, I had changed. I had taken on the persona of Mike Anthony and I didn't like what I had become. I had lost what I had been—the happy-go-lucky kid from Midland, Michigan—and now I knew that I wanted to go back to being Brandon again. But a lot would happen, none of it good, before I got there.

The Bubble Bursts

The week after going 3–11, I went 2–10 on what turned out to be the biggest volume weekend we ever had. Worse, it was the beginning of a long, devastating losing streak. I had never had such a streak before, and I couldn't explain it and didn't know how to handle it. The fact is that if you're going to handicap games every day for a living, you're going to have streaks that run both ways. Periods of near perfection will be followed by stretches of time when you can't buy a winner and there seems to be nothing you can do to turn it around. You study the form and it's as mystifying as it would be if you picked up a book in Braille but you're able to see. You look at the letters and they appear to be familiar but something is wrong and you can't quite decipher it.

That's the same feeling you get when you try to handicap a game while you're on a losing streak. All the figures that once were familiar now seem strange. When you're on a roll, you look at the game and you can see it playing out and it's almost as if a voice whispers in your ear, "Take the Giants minus three." But when you're running downhill, nothing looks right; you doubt every indicator. You might hear the same voice but you no longer trust it. You start digging to prove you're wrong; you become an advocate for the other side and now the other side seems like the right one. You can twist yourself into knots until neither side seems right. And the longer the streak continues, the worse it gets; the mental strain is incredible. It's the closest thing to death that you can imagine.

After the second big losing weekend, clients began to leave us. It was not just the lost business that troubled me. Our clients were real people and they were being hurt because I was sending them in the wrong direction. Some took it harder than others. One afternoon, while visiting my girlfriend in New York, I took a run through Central Park and was greeted by two men. I recognized one as C. M. Novian, a bald, chunky man of middle years, and one of my highest playing clients. I didn't know the other man, but I had seen him before, with Novian, and there was no mistaking the position he filled. He looked like a club fighter who had blocked too many punches with his face and would not mind evening the score, with little regard for who might be the target.

I had met Novian by chance, some months earlier, at a craps table in Las Vegas when I had gone to visit my mother. It was a Monday night and between rolls of the dice I saw him peel off some bills of large denomination and I heard him tell his associate to bet it on Denver minus the points against the L.A. Raiders. I stopped him right there; I looked him straight in the eye and said, "Please don't do that. You might as well just give me the money or go outside and throw it in the air, because you're going to lose it. The Raiders will beat Denver tonight; trust me on that." But he didn't take my advice. He stayed with the Broncos and watched them lose, 23–20. After the game, I was at the craps table again and he approached me.

"How did you know?" he said.

The Bubble Bursts

"Never mind how I knew," I said. "I knew. Give me your number and I'll be in touch and tell you all about it."

I called him when I got home and told him I was Mike Anthony. I had my TV show at the time and I told him to watch it and call me when he was ready. At the end of each show I would give my free play of the week and I was hitting it regularly. He watched the show for seven weeks, during which time my free play of the week went 6–1. In the eighth week, I decided to impress Novian with a major upset. The 3–8 Colts were going into New York to play the Jets. Indy was coming off a 31–0 loss at home to the Chargers, while the Jets had just shut out the Patriots 6–0 on the road. The Jets were installed a double-digit home favorite in what I call a "Vegas reverse trap play"—a losing team off a double-digit home loss facing a winning team off a road win. The world was going to bet the Jets no matter what the number was. On national TV I said the Colts would win the game straight up, which they did, 9–6.

Novian called me right after the game and invited me to visit him at his home on Star Island in South Beach, Florida. His home was nothing less than palatial, the kind of mansion you might expect to be home to a mega-millionaire. He was already betting six figures a game and I asked him for $50,000 up front to get my picks. He didn't hesitate and he made a small fortune during my winning streak. But he later balked when I asked for more money and our relations became less than cordial. When I hit my losing streak, he thought I was holding out my best picks, trying, in effect, to extort more money from him.

So it was a very unhappy duo that greeted me that chilly afternoon in Central Park. Novian had a right to be unhappy. My picks had cost him several million dollars during the losing streak. Now he was here to express his displeasure. His bodyguard put me in a choke hold from behind and Novian asked for an explanation and an apology. He had done his homework. Not only had he found where I lived, he knew about my mother—where she lived and where she worked. He said he could make my life tragic if he was not satisfied with what I had to say.

"What is it you want from me?" I asked. "I'm trying to win. I just can't get out of my own way right now. It's not just you; I'm losing for everyone now. Losing streaks happen. Give me some time to work through this; I'll start winning again."

He could tell that I was sincere. I think he could see that I lived and died with these games and that I would never go into the tank intentionally. Hollywood took some liberties with what happened next. I prefer not to go into detail about what actually occurred but just leave it that I am glad to still be alive today. He left with his bodyguard and I never heard from him again. I had other whales—guys who would bet five and six figures a game—who stayed with me. There was a jeweler in Beverly Hills and a guy in Montana who bet big, but it didn't seem important anymore. I sensed that events were beginning to spin out of control. I was causing people great harm and grinding myself to bits in the process. I hung in there for another year and a half, knowing full well that my time to leave was drawing near. I had opened the 1995 season by losing five straight Monday Night Football games, games that were traditionally the last chance for players who lost with me on Sunday to get even. Now, in week six, after another poor Sunday, I loved the Monday night game and I was going to promote it big-time as a chance for my clients to recoup some of their losses. San Diego was a three-and-a-half-point underdog to the Chiefs in Kansas City, and I liked the Chargers with the points and the under at thirty-seven and a half. I advised straight plays on San Diego and the under plus the parlay as a separate bet. If both sides came in, all of Sunday's debts could be erased and the bettor would be in the black.

Everything was just fine for fifty-eight minutes. At the two-minute warning, San Diego was leading 14–10 and had possession of the ball, fourth-and-goal, at Kansas City's three-yard line. Then Bobby Ross, the Chargers' head coach, elected to go for the chip-shot field goal and San Diego went ahead, 17–10. Joe Montana, the Chiefs' quarterback now in the twilight of his career, did what he always did best. He took his team down the field to score the tying touchdown with twelve seconds left on the clock. With overtime looming, I'm still in good shape. The game figured to be won with a field goal and regardless of which team kicked it I would still beat the spread and stay below the under, winning each bet by half a point. San Diego got the ball to start the overtime, went three

and out, and punted. Tamarick Vanover received the punt
and raced down the left sideline for a touchdown. I lost
the game by a point and a half and the under by two and
a half after it looked like I had both in my pocket with
two minutes to play. It was the toughest double-sided loss
I ever endured. I had wiped out most of my clients and I
felt that I had nothing left. It was the only time in my life
that I felt suicidal. I wanted to put a gun to my head, but
fortunately I didn't own one.

The next day was catastrophic. The most frantic call I
received was from Amir, the dry cleaners owner I met at
Mickey Mantle's, who had become a steady and increasingly heavy bettor. I had taken him from a $50 player to a
guy who was betting as much as $25,000 a game. I made
him a small fortune, and I repeatedly told him to put
some of the money away. "Save some of your winnings,"
I told him. "This won't go on forever. Eventually, I'll hit a
losing streak. It's going to happen." Then, when I started
losing, I told him to cut back. "Stop chasing your losses,"
I told him. "Hold off until I get hot again." But he kept
right on betting at the same level.

The day after the Kansas City–San Diego game he
called, and he was frantic and totally out of control. "I'm
wiped out, Mike," he told me . . . "my business, my house,
my credit. Who the fuck are you? Like this is some kind
of game. I was betting a few thousand dollars a Sunday
when I called you. You pushed me, you destroyed me. I
lost $380,000 this weekend. I was going to get married, I
had a life."

I reminded him that I had warned him to ease up, to exercise money management. "I told you I would go on a losing streak," I said. "It happens. What goes up eventually comes down. Even when I'm hot, I don't win every single day. You have nothing left because you didn't take my advice."

But even as I justified myself, I could feel his pain. Whether I was directly responsible or not, I had helped put him in that position and I knew the end was drawing near for me; I had to get out. When I hung up, with Amir's voice still echoing in my head, I wrote Walt a letter of resignation. I told him it was time for me to leave and go in another direction. I wished him well and said I was sure he would find another Mike Anthony. There was no hostility on my part, but there was plenty on his. He didn't handle it very well. He was insecure and paranoid, and he was sure I was going to work for a competitor. I never spoke to him directly about it, but other salesmen called and told me he was ready to give me whatever I wanted. He paged me eighty-two times in two days, but I didn't take the calls. I was done and there was no point in discussing it. I got in my car and headed west. I was going home, to my family in Las Vegas, and I would try to get a handle on my future while traversing the country.

My experience with Walter had been instructive; I learned a great deal about myself, and I began to take inventory of some of my assets. Now in my mid-thirties and looking to the future, I understood that my success at handicapping and selling my opinions embraced two aspects of my character—a commitment to detail in making my picks and a salesman's gift for selling them. At a very young age, I had learned that sales is no more than personality. If you seem genuine, if you make people laugh, if they like you when they meet you, you can sell them most anything. The trait that feeds personality is confidence, and together they form a potent combination. I had a degree of confidence when I was younger, particularly when it came to playing sports, but it was always shaded by a little bit of doubt. Now I had a quiet self-assurance that was unshakeable. Being Mike Anthony had boosted my sense of self and polished my speaking skills. The gift of gab came naturally to me; I had learned how to harness it and when to put it to work over the past few years. Playing Mike Anthony had been the perfect training ground. As I drove across the country, I had no clear idea of where I would end up or what I would be doing, but I felt that whatever my future held, I would be ready to embrace it.

The drive west was long enough to leave room for many changes of mood. I was fully aware of what I was walking away from, but I had not yet completely digested it. I had become arguably the number one sports handicapper in the country. People were betting hundreds of thousands of dollars on my opinion, and while that was gratifying, it was also a considerable weight to carry every day of the year. The pressure at times was unbearable. But the life I was living would not be easy to duplicate. I had everything a thirty-two-year-old kid from Midland,

Michigan, could want—lots of money, gorgeous women, a Porsche—everything. It was a lot to leave behind, but once I made the decision it was as if a thousand-pound elephant had been lifted from my shoulders. I was able to breathe again; I felt alive again. I had recently moved from New York to Atlanta, Georgia, as a first step to breaking the connection, and that made leaving a bit easier. I sold just about everything I owned. I had acquired some very nice art work, and I sold it all, along with my furniture—my couches, my bed, my big-screen TVs, everything. I sold it all to one guy for $12,000, although it was probably worth five times that. The only thing I took with me was my clothes. I traded in my Porsche for a Ford Explorer, loaded it up, and set out on my drive cross-country.

I knew that breaking away would not be a simple matter, and it wasn't long before I learned just how right I was. My pager nearly exploded. Cell phones were not yet in vogue in 1995; pagers were the way you got hold of people on the run and mine was working overtime. The word spread quickly that I had left Walter, and people in the industry were trying to reach me. I did not feel up to discussing my situation at the time. I tossed the pager out the window and kept on driving. It was a relief to have that elephant off my back, but there was nothing to replace it and I was left with an empty feeling. "What are you going to do now?" I asked myself. "You had a secure job that paid very well; you never had to worry about money, never had to worry about anything. What are you going to do now?"

The biggest mistake I had made while working for Walter was that I didn't save any money. I spent what I made as though all I had to do was step outside on my front lawn and pick new bills from the trees. Spending money recklessly was probably my worst attribute. I'm sure I picked the habit up from Walter, who tossed money around as if it were in endless supply. Now, reality had begun to set in. I had $12,000, but it was not going to last very long. What was I going to do when the money ran out? Was I going to be a host in a Vegas casino? Was I going to continue my relationship with the world of sports gambling? I had no idea where my life was going or what there was out there for me. What I did know was that I felt free. I was free mentally, physically, spiritually, emotionally, and that feeling was enough to sustain me throughout the drive.

I remember stopping at a hotel that first night on my way to Vegas. It was a Wednesday and there was an NBA game on TV. I had no stake in the game but as I watched it I wanted to know what the line was. If I didn't know the line I didn't feel like watching the game. I turned off the TV and I knew right then that I would have to find a way to detach myself completely. I was heading for Las Vegas, but that was not the place to be if I was going to get away from the scene. Sports gambling had an attraction that was not always easy to resist. It was, after all, a massive industry that was as complex and multi-faceted as any other big business. It had a long and colorful history, which made it all the more intriguing because a large part of it thrived in the shadows and found its home in corners that existed outside of the law.

A BRIEF HISTORY OF SPORTS GAMBLING

Betting on sporting events is probably as old as the events themselves. There are no official records of when or how it began, but evidence suggests that when the Greeks played the games that later became the Olympics, people were betting on the outcome. We know for certain that betting on baseball games was a popular pastime in the early part of the twentieth century and very likely had started from the game's professional beginnings, shortly after the Civil War. We know too that there was much speculation that prominent players such as Ty Cobb, Tris

Speaker, and Hal Chase were suspected of accepting bribes on occasion to play less than their best. Such speculation was given added credibility in 1919 when eight players on the Chicago White Sox were found to have dumped the World Series in what became known as the Black Sox scandal. The mastermind of that fix, still the most notorious in sports history, was a criminal genius by the name of Arnold Rothstein.

A product of New York's Lower East Side and raised an Orthodox Jew in a middle-class German Jewish family, Rothstein developed an early taste for the other side of the street. At a precociously young age, he was already involved in every form of white-collar criminal activity, including bootlegging, loan-sharking, narcotics, and of course gambling. Rothstein loved everything about gambling except the risk that was involved. He therefore did what he could to eliminate that aspect of the proposition. Chance was for suckers. Like Willie Sutton, who said he robbed banks because that's where the money was, Rothstein knew to go where the money was, and he knew exactly how to game the system. Known variously as "the Big Bankroll," "Mr. Big," "the Man Uptown," and "the Fixer," he was referred to by his confederates simply as A. R. By 1915, Rothstein had become the godfather of organized crime, and big-time gambling would be the cornerstone of his legacy.

The two innovations that made sports betting a popular pastime and a big business were the vigorish and the point spread. The term "vigorish" comes from the Russian word "vyigrysh," which means "winnings," but it is unclear when it was introduced to betting or where the idea came from. The vig, which is the equal of the commission earned by a broker in a stock transaction, enabled bookmakers to take unlimited action on a game without concern for going broke if the wrong side won. By taking approximately equal amounts on both sides of the game, a bookie could assure himself a profit derived from the ten percent margin paid by the losing side. The hazard that remained was the possibility that the action on one side would be far greater than the amount bet on the other so that the bookmaker would, in effect, be wagering on the team that did not draw much backing. The solution was a procedure in which bookmakers "laid off" some of the wagers on the more heavily bet team with bookies whose action favored the other side.

Of course there were no guarantees. Inevitably, there were games in which the betting line seemed to be off and every bookie in town was deluged with bets on the same team. An example was the 1985 season Super Bowl between the Chicago Bears and the New England Patriots. The Bears had gone 15–1 during the regular season and opened a heavy favorite. But even getting double digits, the Pats were an unattractive bet. The line inched up slowly during the two weeks before the game. In some quarters, it opened at nine and a half, moved to ten, and finally as high as twelve. Still, the money poured in on Chicago, but the bookies could not move the line any higher for fear of being "middled." The two and a half point middle between nine and a half and twelve was enormously risky for a bookmaker. For if a large sum were bet on the Bears giving nine and a half points and a similarly large sum were bet on the Pats getting twelve, both sides would win if the final score fell somewhere in the middle, the Bears winning by either by ten or eleven points. Hitting a "middle" was a bookmaker's nightmare. As it turned out, the result was not quite a nightmare, more like a bad dream. The Bears devastated New England, 46–10. The betting handle never came close to evening out, not even with the line move, and the bookmakers paid out a bundle in Bears money.

As important as vigorish was in the advance of sports betting, it was the development of the point spread that made the real difference. The point spread, sometimes referred to as the "line," is the margin by which one team is expected to beat the other. No one seems to know for certain who first came up with the idea, but the name most often suggested is that of Charles McNeil, a professor at the University of Chicago, who applied his mathematical skill to both the stock market and the sports scene. It is fairly clear, however, that the point spread made its appearance in the late thirties or early forties. Until then, bettors were simply offered straight odds on a game, but unless the odds were very close, 2-to-1 or less, the action was likely to be slow. It is an axiom of gambling that betting odds are sweets for the sucker. It does not matter how good the odds are if your team loses. Conversely, if one wishes to put his money on a heavy favorite, 6-to-1 for example, he finds he must make a substantial investment on the chance of winning a rather small sum. As a consequence, few bettors were prepared to risk their money on a game between two mismatched teams. Bookmakers, for their part, operated at great peril. If the odds were set too low, there would be little action on the game. If they were too high, they would encourage fortune hunters to invest small amounts on the chance of hitting it big. In such a case, if a real long shot came in, a bookie could be put out of business. The invention of the point spread, in one fell swoop, settled all the issues, for with the spread, every game became, theoretically, an even money proposition.

The first point spreads covered a three-point range. A team might be quoted as a six-eight favorite, which meant that the favorite would have to win by eight points or more for the bettor to collect, while a bet on the underdog would be good if it lost by six or fewer. It was the middle point that was the killer, for if the favorite won by seven points, all bets were lost. Bettors were quick to discern the hazards of the system. An unusually large number of games seemed to hit the middle; nobody won. And so an adjustment was made. Only one point line was given, usually with a half point, or a "hook," tacked on to avert a tie or, in gambler's parlance, a "push." Thus if a team was a seven-and-a-half-point favorite, it would have to win by eight for its backers to collect. If it won by seven or fewer, it was a payday for the underdog. Now, every team had a legitimate chance to "win" by beating the line. The point spread was the great equalizer.

Basketball and football were on their way to becoming the most heavily bet sports in America (except, of course, for horse racing). The spread was the gambler's delight and balm for the bookmaker; it made every game a toss-up. Other possibilities were also introduced. Given the point spread, a team could win a game on the board while losing it to the spread. High-stakes gamblers recognized an opportunity when they saw one. They could conceivably take some of the risk out of gambling by offering to share their winnings with some of the players they bet on. The players after all would not be dumping a game; they would merely be shaving the points. What difference did it make whether they won by seven points or four?

It did not take long for the possibility to emerge as reality. In 1945, just a few years after the single point spread came into use, five Brooklyn College players admitted having accepted bribes to manipulate the score of a basketball game. A year later, on the eve of the NFL championship game between the Giants and the Bears, it was discovered that two Giants players, quarterback Frank Filchock and fullback Merle Hapes, had been made similar offers by gamblers. Other incidents followed until 1951, when the bubble finally burst with a college basketball point-shaving scandal that dwarfed, in duration and scope, the 1919 Black Sox endeavor. It involved dozens of players from colleges in New York and the Midwest, and yet it was only a hint of what was uncovered ten years later when college teams from coast to coast were implicated in a massive point-shaving operation.

The prospect that the outcome of some games might be determined before they were played did nothing to slake the appetite of bettors. The volume of sports gambling continued to increase. Practical reason suggested that fixes grew less likely as the lid came off salaries paid to the players in the NBA and NFL. How much might a gambler be ready to offer by way of a bribe to an athlete who is earning $10 or $20 million a year? As for big-time college players, why would they risk the fortune awaiting them when they left college, perhaps after only a year or two? The most visible targets for a bribe now might be the officials who referee the games. One such incident involving an NBA official occurred in 2007. Suspicions have been voiced regarding some NFL officiating in recent years, but not the slightest degree of evidence has been introduced. All the same, it is not unheard of for the outcome of a game to be decided by a bad call, whether intentional or simply the product of human error.

Regardless of the cause, as many bettors are likely to profit from the call as those who will be its victims, and so the volume of money gambled, both legally and illegally, continues to grow. On the day of a big game, a Las Vegas sports book bears a close resemblance to the floor of a big-city stock exchange, and the mood is just as frantic. Nearly $1 billion is wagered legally in Nevada on the Super Bowl, and a good bit more during the two-plus weeks of March Madness. All told, Nevada sports books handle well over $3 billion a year. Estimates of how much is bet illegally vary wildly. Conservative figures suggest that perhaps 75 percent of bets are made illegally; other approximations go as high as 99 percent. A 1999 report by the National Gaming Impact Study Commission esti-mated that illegal sports gambling accounted for as much as $380 billion a year, with 40 million Americans wagering $6 billion every weekend during the twenty-week pro and college football season. Those figures have increased dramatically with the advent of offshore betting on the Internet. The total wagered each year now might run as high as half a trillion dollars.

So it was a thriving industry that I was leaving behind when I walked out on Walter in the fall of 1995. I always believed I might eventually go back to it, but at the time I knew I had to let it go. What I was yet to come to grips with was that I had no idea what might replace it.

—S. C.

CHAPTER

9

THE FUTURE BECKONS

A whole world of possibilities stretched out before me, but I wasn't headed in any particular direction. I just knew I had to get away from what I'd been doing. I needed a change of scenery and to find something that would get my mind off of handicapping sporting events. I thought it would be a good idea to get out of the country for a while, and the first spot that came to mind was, of all places, Australia. Why Australia? One, I had never been there; two, it was very far away; and three, I had always wanted to go scuba diving off the Great Barrier Reef. I had read about it, and when I was working at the Nevada Sports Schedule, the scorephone announcer, Danny Guess, used to talk about going to Australia. Going there became a common goal for both of us. Danny and I worked the Saturday night shift, which was the busiest of all, and we became great friends. We'd sit there at the station, and when the shift was winding down, we'd tune to a West Coast game and talk about going to Australia together. We researched the trip and planned it out; we knew exactly where we were going to go and what we were going to do; and then Danny jumped ship. He met a girl, got married, had kids, and I went to New York to work for Walter. So we never realized the dream of going to Australia together, but I knew that I would do it myself some day. I knew I would go Down Under and scuba dive off the Great Barrier Reef, and I was certain that the time was now.

So I spent a few weeks with my mom and family in Vegas and then took off for Australia by myself. I took my golf clubs and enough clothing with the idea of staying from six months to a year. I landed in Sydney, found a place to stay, and began to try to work things out. I was living the way I had always lived my life, by the seat of my pants, not knowing where I was going or how I was going to get there. But I knew that one way or another, I'd find my way. In the meantime, it felt good being by myself in Australia where no one recognized me and there was no pressure to do anything but what I felt like doing.

I remember hanging out at Bondi Beach, which was the place to be down there, chatting with the bartenders, listening to the Australian accents, and enjoying the Australian women who loved American men because we were so much more polite than the natives. The two bartenders were brothers and I got to know them pretty well and they liked listening to my stories. "What are you doing down here?" they wanted to know. "You're by yourself, you don't know anyone, why are you here, what are you doing?" I began to tell them the story of my life. I told them about handicapping, picking games on which people bet hundreds of thousands of dollars. I told them about bad beats and good beats, and they couldn't get enough of it. They loved hearing about games coming down to the wire. I would give the accounts as if I were broadcasting the games, and they would stop what they were doing, waiting to hear their outcomes; did my team cover or not? They were fascinated by the amount of money that was riding on these games. The more I told them, the more they wanted to hear.

One day, one of them said to me, "You know, your life would make a great movie." And with that, a light went on inside my head. It was like that moment in the film *Rocky II,* where Adrienne leans over and whispers in Rocky's ear, "Just win," and it was as if destiny had spoken to him. Right then, I knew that was what I had to do. I was going to have a movie made of my life, and once I set my mind to it, nothing was going to stop me. I had no idea at the time how I would go about it. I knew it was a long shot. But now I had something to focus on. For the time being, I remained in Australia and enjoyed the scenery, the people, and the freedom to do what I wanted to do whenever I wanted to do it. I had $12,000 or so from my days with Walter so I was not faced with a financial crunch. The hotel I was staying at was modestly priced and I was renting by the week. The hotel bar, where I spent a good deal of time just hanging out, was down at the beach, which made everything very convenient. I stayed in shape playing pickup basketball in an informal league that was run by the bartender brothers.

It was a good life, but after a month or so, somewhat to my surprise, I began to feel homesick. There was a movie, *The American President*, with Michael Douglas, which was playing down there, and I watched it eleven straight days because it took me back to the United States. For added measure, I now had a goal I was looking toward. Once the idea of making a movie of my life was planted, I could not put it out of my mind. I was getting restless and after six weeks in Sydney I knew it was time to go. I caught a Greyhound bus and rode it for forty-eight hours to Cairns, where the Great Barrier Reef is located. I scuba dived the reef, fulfilling a long-held dream, did some skydiving while there, and now it was time to move ahead in pursuit of my next dream.

On the flight home, I looked back on the time I spent in Australia with much pleasure. I've always said that life is about experiences, both good and bad. The good ones you take with you and the bad ones you leave behind. I had nothing but fond memories of my stay in Sydney—sitting with the bartenders, just talking about this and that; being nobody that anyone expects something from; feeling no pressure about picking games or worrying about how much money people are betting on my opinions. I even learned a bit about cricket and rugby. I watched some cricket matches, and the bartenders explained the action to me, but I never really got the hang of it. I couldn't figure how you might handicap a game or what the odds might be. But I enjoyed learning as much as I did. And then, of course, the climax was scuba diving the Great Barrier Reef. I ended my brief sojourn on that note, and now I was ready to move forward.

Getting a movie made of my life had become my great American Dream and I was thinking about how to make my first move in that direction. While I wasn't sure how to get started, I knew where I would have to be to further my chances. I stopped first in Las Vegas to visit with my mom. I stayed for about a month, then told her it would be a while before I saw her again; I was bound for Los Angeles.

It was early in 1996 when I got to L.A. Actually, I settled in El Segundo, which was right next to the Los Angeles International Airport. I had met some people who rented me a room, and it was in an ideal location. It was fifteen minutes from the Spectrum Club in Manhattan Beach. The Spectrum was a health club and it was where college and NBA players went to play some hoops during the off-season. If they weren't playing at UCLA's Pauley Pavilion on the weekend, you would find them at the Spectrum playing pickup games. One afternoon I found myself guarding and being guarded by Lisa Leslie, the women's All-American and Olympic hero, and with the score tied I crossed over and drained a game winner. She was a tough defender; she made you work for everything you got and more than held her own against the men. But on this occasion I managed to get some space and nail the jumper.

It was at the Spectrum that I ran into a young man by the name of Brian Wirth, who was a tennis pro at the Riviera Country Club. I had met him years ago when I was living in L.A. after getting out of the navy. At the time, I was working as a bouncer at a bar two nights a week and I told him I was looking for a job, preferably in the sports field. I had tried to line something up at the Spectrum but nothing was available. He said he might be able to get me a spot working in the coordinator's office at the Riviera tennis club. Coordinators are responsible for assigning courts to members, setting up matches, and keeping track of the schedule. Brian asked me if I would be interested and I told him, absolutely. I was looking for any kind of job and as the weeks went by I was becoming more and more desperate. Even then, I was certain that at some point in my life I would go back to handicapping. I was 100 percent sure of that, but it wasn't time yet. I wanted to hold on to my freedom a while longer, and of course there was that dream I was pursuing. The movie remained in the forefront of my mind, and I believed I was in the right location to get it moving, but in the meantime I was in need of a job.

As it developed, I was about to take my first step toward satisfying both aims.

Brian sent me to the Riviera Country Club where I was interviewed for the coordinator's job. I had played some tennis in my youth and I knew the game well enough. I also got along well with people and that combination made me well suited for the job; I soon learned the job was right for me as well. I was hired on the spot, and it didn't take me long to realize that I had struck gold. This was break number one on the road to my goal.

The job itself was a piece of cake. Club members would call for an appointment; I would find a court that was open at around the time they wanted to play and often I was asked to hook them up with another player who wanted a game. The only aspect of the job that was more than mechanical was matching the players. James Bell, for one, might be looking for someone to play with. I knew that Bell was on his way to playing college tennis and that he was one of the best players at the club, and so I needed to find someone who could at least give him a game. I remember sitting in the coordinator's office with James on Friday nights, and he would be talking about Nicole Richie, telling me that he'd been inviting her and her friends to come down to the Riviera. On many a Friday night, actor Dabney Coleman would come by after everyone left and hit serves in the dark with only a street light offering illumination. I missed those times. I loved the job and I loved being at the Riviera. In a way it was like revisiting a bit of my past. I remembered walking the Riviera golf course when I was in the navy and telling myself that I had to play it some day. I had watched the Nissan Open there, and I could see that the course was special and I wanted to return to it. Now here I was working at the club. Although the tennis courts were well off to the left of the golf course, it was, as I said, the first step.

The next break came my way a few months later when I met Gordon Grah, the assistant head golf pro, who was dating one of the members of the tennis staff. Grah asked me if I played basketball. I said I did and he invited me to play on Mondays and Wednesdays at a private gym that was rented by one of his golfing members, Tom Hacker. Tom was in the mortgage business; he had a number of properties and he dabbled in the stock market. So now I'm playing basketball twice a week with businessmen who are movers and shakers at the golf club. I was the most accomplished player on the court and attracted some attention. Grah and I were becoming somewhat friendly and an interesting network was beginning to form.

My next connection, like so many others, came by way of a chance meeting while watching a basketball game at a bar. One Saturday in the fall of 1996, driving home from the tennis club, I stopped at Jerry's Deli in Marina del Rey and took a seat at the bar to get a quick bite to eat. The Washington State–UCLA basketball game was on TV and the gentleman to my right obviously had some action on the game. I leaned over and asked him which side he had. He had Washington State plus nine and a half and they were trailing by fourteen at the start of the second half. He said it didn't look good, and I said to him, "Are you crazy? You're right where you want to be. UCLA will open their lead to about eighteen points, and with a few minutes left they'll pull their starters, Washington State will hit a few threes and you'll have your cover." I knew that State had some good outside shooters and that down by double digits with time running out they would be looking to take a quick route to get back in the game. "Relax," I said, "you want to stress out, then wait until we're at the five-minute mark. When it comes to the spread, almost all of these games are decided in the last five minutes."

All the while, I noticed that there was a gentleman sitting to the right of this guy who seemed to be paying very close attention to our conversation. Sure enough, inside of five minutes UCLA goes up by eighteen and State hits a couple of threes to cut the Bruins lead to twelve. State begins fouling and UCLA misses a couple of front-end free throws on one-and-ones. State is down by ten with thirty seconds left, but a quick three gets them within seven. They call time out with twenty-eight seconds to go and foul on the in-bounds pass. UCLA hits both foul shots to move ahead by nine, half a point under the spread. With eighteen seconds left Washington State misses a three and commits a foul. UCLA makes both ends and the lead goes to eleven. State has one more chance and they make good on it; they drop in a three at the buzzer, lose by eight and my bar pal covers his bet. The guy wants to know how I nailed it so close, and for a moment I was about to go into my Mike Anthony routine, but I decided to let it go. There was a part of me that would always be Mike Anthony, but at least for the time being I had put it behind me and I said, "I'm just a sports fan; I follow these things closely."

He leaves with a smile on his face, but the man who was sitting next to him was interested in pursuing it. His name is Mark O'Brien and he worked for Warner Bros. He sold television sitcoms for reruns, or something of that nature. I told him I had an idea for a movie and we got to talking about movies and the entertainment business in general. He told me that I would have to write a film treatment and register with the Writers Guild if I wanted to write a movie script and we began to explore other avenues of interest. Out of nowhere, I told him I also had thoughts of becoming an actor. He told me the first thing I would have to do to get started in that direction was to get myself some head shots. Then I'd have to find an agent and start the auditioning process all actors go through—commercials, independent movies—just to get used to the routine.

In a way, I had been an actor all my life. What else was I doing when I was playing Mike Anthony? I had created a character and I portrayed him to the point where I could hardly tell the difference between him and me. I had never really thought of becoming a professional actor, but everything in the Hollywood area seems to revolve around the movie industry. So many people around you are in the business in one capacity or another that you get the feeling that you belong there too. The Riviera was teeming with agents, producers, writers, and I began to think, why not?

The Future Beckons

An actor, a screenwriter, the subject of a movie—any one of them, maybe all three. I had always been a dreamer, and if you're going to dream, why not dream big?

O'Brien did nothing to discourage me. He introduced me to a friend of his, Tammy Chase, who was a manager for a big company in the talent-hunt business. Tammy said that the way to get started was to try to land a job in a television commercial, and she got right on the case. She put me in touch with an agent at Commercials Unlimited, Richard Reiner, who was the nephew of Carl Reiner and the cousin of Rob, both Hollywood luminaries. Richard and I connected immediately. I gave him the *Reader's Digest* version of my life story, highlighted by my days as Mike Anthony. I also brought him a tape of my television show with me talking about betting lines, winners and losers, and everything else that went with it. Richard was impressed and so was another agent he introduced me to, by the name of Randi Rubenstein. After spending thirty minutes with me, Randi paid me what to this day is one of the greatest compliments I've ever received: "You have one of the most genuine personalities I have ever met and you are going to do great in this town." She said, "Let's sign him up," and within a matter of hours I had an appointment to audition for a national Boston Market chicken commercial. I drove back to El Segundo from Beverly Hills, put on a suit, and headed for the Valley where the commercial studio was.

The audition was fun and it went very well. The following week, Richard called me and said I had a callback for a second audition. A few days later, he called again and said I had another callback; I was down to the final five. But that's as far as I got; that's as far as I ever got. Richard was encouraged by my early success. Getting to the final five the first time out of the box was considered more than slightly promising. So Richard set me up to get more headshots, he got me a commercial agent, and I began going out on auditions regularly, but I never got anywhere close again. In the process, I realized that actors, other than the name-brand few, must deal constantly with rejection, and I wasn't made for that. I suppose it's a character defect of sorts, but I always took things personally even when there was no personal affront intended. The string of rejections was beginning to get to me.

Another aspect of the auditions was beginning to get to me as well. I would get sent out for a role, and Richard would tell me, "This is absolutely perfect for you; it's for Pinnacle Golf." So I would go up for the audition and there would be 250 guys waiting in the reception area and none of them looked anything like me. Some of them were short or fat, some were a lot older than me, others much younger. I would call Richard and say, "These guys look nothing like me; how was I perfect for that?" But they just keep sending you out; you never know when you might get lucky. You hit enough golf balls and one day you might get a hole-in-one. I knew this was not the route to my movie goal. I had to spin it another way. Early in their careers, Matt Damon and Ben Affleck were getting acting jobs but they weren't being taken seriously, so they decided to take matters into their own hands. They wrote *Good Will Hunting* not only because it was a great story, but also because it would be a showcase for their acting skills. With that, they rose right to the top. I decided to follow their lead.

I had been thinking about writing my own treatment for a movie, and I remembered what Mark O'Brien had told me about registering it to protect myself. I spoke to some people about how you go about it and I registered with the Writers Guild. In the scenario I developed, I was a salesman working for Walter in the boiler room and I had a client who's betting hundreds of thousands of dollars. I never met him but he had a very distinct voice that I recognized but couldn't place. Gradually, the theme began to evolve into a film that was not my life story, but a political thriller based on my work as a handicapper. I titled it *Point Spread*. The story went like this:

One night I'm watching the news on television and I recognize the voice of my big-money player and there on the screen is the governor of Virginia, who is a serious candidate for the presidency of the United States. The next day, I hook up recording equipment and start taping every conversation I have with him. The plot takes its first turn when I go on a losing streak and during a conversation in which the governor is expressing his dissatisfaction, I let his name slip out. He hangs up the phone, but now he knows that I know who he is. He is a compulsive gambler who is betting huge sums of money illegally with a bookmaker, not the wisest course of action for a man seeking the presidency.

The governor, of course, is well connected and what follows is an action sequence in which the Mob tries unsuccessfully to get the tapes, there is a failed attempt on my life, and I am taken hostage and forced to make a pick in a basketball game with my life riding on the outcome. I'm tied to a chair in front of a TV set, watching the game and sweating out the result in the same way my clients often sweated it out after betting heavily on my picks. It all ends happily. My team covers and I help the FBI nail the governor and the Mob, who are trying to blackmail him with tapes so they will own him when he gets elected.

In brief, that was the treatment. I showed it to one of the tennis players at the club who was a film producer. He said he liked it but he turned it down, and I found that that was not an unusual response. Everyone I showed it to said they liked the idea but for one reason or another, they rejected it. It was much the same as auditioning. Everyone thought you were great but you never got the job. I was back to the routine of rejection. But then something happened. Out of nowhere, Gordon Grah tells me that they need some caddies at the golf club. He asks if I'm interested. Was I interested? I had been in Los Angeles for a year and at the club for nine months. It was March of 1997, and my life was about to take a turn due north.

CONNECTING ON THE LINKS

W hen I went to the caddy shack for the first time, I felt like I had just stepped over the threshold into my future. Inside, waiting to be called, was a cast of characters that could not easily be described—wannabe actors and rock stars, recovering addicts, lots of Mexicans just trying to scratch out a living. The particular character I was interested in seeing was an assistant golf pro by the name of Kris Gundmunson. Kris wanted to take me out to see if I knew my way around a golf course.

I had played the Riviera course three or four times in the nine months I had been working there and I knew it pretty well; I was familiar with the nuances of the greens and where the hazards were located. We went nine holes and Kris said, "You're just fine," so now I was exactly where I had hoped to be. I gave myself a three-year time frame. If I didn't connect with a film producer in that time I was going to go back to handicapping. I continued to watch the lines and handicap the games informally, trying to stay up to date on the various sports.

It took a while to get started. Caddying is a line of work that carries with it no guarantees. You can spend quite a few days sitting in the caddy shack without getting a job, and that's exactly what I did. My career as a caddy started early on a Tuesday morning and I sat there all that day and the next and went home without having worked at all. I never moved, just sat there putting in my time, showing that I was serious. I was prepared to do that every day of the week until something broke. Aside from looking for a contact, there was big money to be made at the Riviera Golf Club, and I knew things would work out if I remained patient. There was a routine to be followed and there were no shortcuts, at least not yet. Here's how it worked:

You got to the golf starter, Mike Cruz, at 6:20 AM near the first tee and there was a morning draw which was run like a lottery. Senior caddies—those who had been there a year or more—got the first draw; whoever was left took part in a second draw. If ten seniors showed up, they drew from numbers one through ten. Whoever picked number one got the first job of the day, right out of the box. Then the non-seniors drew; whoever drew number one would

Me and Kenny. Every kid should have a best friend like him growing up.

There are four sure things in life: death, taxes, I don't lose Super Bowls, and I will always be able to shoot a basketball.

Me and John Madden share a moment at the
Marriott in New York City.

Under the 16-inch guns
of the *New Jersey*.

Me and Rock on the USS
New Jersey.

Me and former President Clinton. I would have gotten the picture right next to him but the secret service didn't like my club selection on the first hole.

Me and Tiger. I just told him that I saw him hit it to within 2 feet at the Navy course on the par 3 when he was eight years old. Best swing I ever saw.

Me, Tiger, and Ted Tryba on the 4th tee box during Sunday's final round of the 1999 Nissan Open. Tiger was super cool to hang with inside the ropes that day until the back 9 when things got serious.

Ted and me on the 18th hole during Saturday's historic round. Maybe we should have hit 9-iron there, but I guess we'll never know.

Me and soap star Eric Braeden clowning around at the Riviera Tennis Club. My mom's favorite soap star and a heckuva tennis player.

Me, Dustin Hoffman and Rene Russo. The first team that believed in me. I am truly grateful to have had their support.

Me, Matthew McConaughey, and Al Pacino on the set of
Two for the Money in New York City. A day to remember.

Me, Mom, and my brother Bryan before heading to the premiere.

Working the red carpet at the *Two for the Money* premiere. An experience of a lifetime to say the least.

Me and director D.J. Caruso at the premiere.

Me, Dan Gilroy, and Rene. The two of the most sincere and genuine people I have ever met.

Me, Venus, and Serena Williams at the premiere.

Me, Rene, and producer Jay Cohen at the premiere.

Me and Matt at the after party sharing a laugh. Couldn't have had a better guy play me.

Me, my best friend Tommy O'Connell, and Matt.

Me, Dr. J, and Michael Barkann on the set of *Daily News Live* in Philadelphia.

Me and Coach Hursey at Crystal Downs Country Club. It's an honor to not only call him coach but a great friend as well.

Me and my gorgeous wife, Kim. Definitely out-kicked my coverage on that one.

Teeing it up at the Plantation course in Kapalua, Hawaii on my honeymoon. Life is good.

get the eleventh job of the day, and so on. Cruz would show you the worksheet for the day with all the jobs that had been booked. If the sheet was full, there was a good chance you would work at least once, and if you were a senior caddy you would have the option of working a second loop with a good draw. For example, if you pulled number one, you would probably be on the course by 7 AM and you would be done no later than 11:30. You could grab a quick bite to eat and be back out again in the afternoon. Working two loops, you might make as much as $300 cash that day and that's a big day.

On my sixth day, Sunday afternoon at around 2 PM, after all the other caddies had worked, I got my first call. Someone came in and told me there was a single bag. A single bag means you're caddying for just one player; the player is going to play the course by himself. You carry his bag, have all his yardage to the green for his approach shots, and it is essential that you are confident that the information you give him is correct. If he has not played the course regularly, you point out the hazards along the way and, the biggest key for a caddy at a course like the Riviera, you read the greens for him; does a green break left or right and how sharp is the break? Any PGA player will tell you that the Riviera has some of the toughest greens to read on the tour. That's where a good caddy earns his money.

So my first job was a single bag and the guy whose bag I was carrying was Robbie Krieger's, the guitarist for the Doors. It was just him and me for eighteen holes and it was great. Robbie's father had been a member of the Riviera for many years, so Robbie had grown up playing the course and he was a good golfer; he had a beautiful swing. He also liked company when he played and he enjoyed talking. He spoke about Jim Morrison, the Doors' lead singer, about his demons and how he died under largely unknown circumstances at the age of twenty-seven. He gave me the whole history of how the group was formed and how they rose to fame. He was an unbelievably nice guy—straightforward and genuine. Walking up to the eighteenth hole, he handed me $60, a $40 single-bag fee and a $20 tip. I felt like I had just won the lotto. On my first job, I had spent four hours alone with Robbie Krieger, chatting as though we were old friends. I felt it was an omen. Walking back to the caddy shack and on the Culver City green bus on my way back to El Segundo, I remember thinking that my dream about the movie was destined to become reality. On that March day in 1997, I knew it would all come together. One way or another—actor, producer, agent, whatever—the dream would come true; I was going to cover the spread. I believed it with 100 percent conviction. If I broke my maiden with Robbie Krieger, you never knew who else might be on the horizon at this lottery of all lotteries, this cavalcade of Hollywood bigwigs, entertainers, producers, writers. It was as if I were taking part in a huge grab bag; I couldn't guess what I might pull out next, but I knew there was an assortment of wonders inside the bag and there was no way I could lose.

I was still floating on air the next day, but I soon returned to a more sober reality. I couldn't expect to get a celebrity every day, but the Riviera was a gold mine, and while you were waiting you could make a helluva lot of money. I was a hustler, a salesman, I knew how to make things happen. When I got a player I knew nothing about I would try talking sports with him to see if he was a bettor. If he was, and I could give him a little inside information, there would often be something extra in it for me at the end of the round. Now and then, someone would say, "You look familiar," and I knew the only place he could have seen me was on television as Mike Anthony. I asked one guy who recognized me, "Who do you like this week?" He told me he liked Denver giving three and a half at Kansas City, and I was sure it was the wrong side. I told him the Chiefs were tough at home and gave him some stats to prove it, and he began picking my brain for other insights. Here he was with a caddy who had just given him a great read on the ninth hole—it went right to left—and he was ready to listen to anything I had to tell him. Also, he was aware that people had paid to get my opinion on a game and he felt he was getting something for nothing.

So I was making out pretty well financially, having a good time along the way, and building myself a reputation at the club. I was beginning to meet the members and they were getting a feel for me and the way I approached caddying. Some of them asked for me specifically. Regardless of what your draw was, if a member requests you, his request was usually honored. It sometimes created difficulties with the other guys in the shack who were waiting for a job. You might be way down on the draw but the phone rings and you're on your way to the first hole while senior caddies are sitting and waiting. It was not a situation that made for popularity, but I wasn't planning to run for office. If I was good enough to be requested, that was my profit and I was happy to get it. I didn't say much to anybody during my first few weeks at the club, but there were a few caddies that I became somewhat friendly with.

One of them was Frank Weatherwax. Frank was a scratch golfer and one of the most senior caddies at the Riviera. He probably could have made the PGA tour (and did compete in a few local qualifying tournaments) but it just didn't happen for him. We would go out on Monday mornings when caddies got to play and I would watch him carry his own bag and without even warming up he would shoot a sixty-seven as if it were nothing. Frank had grown up in Hollywood. His father was the original trainer of the dog Lassie, and he had gone to school with Sean Penn, Charlie Sheen, and Emilio Estevez. Frank recognized me as Mike Anthony; he used to watch my Saturday morning shows. "All this time I'd been trying to place you," he said. "I used to watch your show right here in the caddy shack." Frank took me under his wing, spread my growing legend, you might say, and helped get me more requests. I was certain that if a Hollywood personality came his way he would funnel him in my direction. That put me another step ahead, but my big push forward came from the starter, Mike Cruz. I got to know Mike really well, and our relationship paid dividends for both of us.

I had been at the Riviera just over a month when Mike called me and said, "I have a job for you. These are big money guys and they asked for a caddy with some personality. I like the way you work and I know they'll take good care of you." And they did. They rode a cart and I carried the four putters and, between 8 AM and 1 PM, I made $350. The other caddies in the shack didn't appreciate my being singled out for big-money jobs, but it didn't bother me; I had bigger plans. I went over to Mike after the loop, thanked him for getting me the job, and gave him $100. I doubt that any caddy had ever shared a tip with him before, and he asked me to have dinner with him that night. We met in a Mexican restaurant on Wilshire Boulevard in Santa Monica, and over dinner we basically formulated a plan to run the golf course at the Riviera Country Club together. Mike would hook me up with the big-money groups and I would give him a percentage of the tips. The arrangement worked well for both of us. Over the next few years I caddied for Bill Clinton, Michael Jordan, Wayne Gretzky, Jack Nicholson, Sylvester Stallone, Tom Cruise, Troy Aikman, Marcus Allen, Dennis and Randy Quaid, Dennis Hopper, and Jim Irsay, the owner of the Indianapolis Colts, who, as it turned out, was one of my top three tippers ever.

Mike and I cut our deal in June, and I began making serious money. I was able to move from El Segundo closer to the Riviera, which was in the Pacific Palisades section of Los Angeles. Tom Hacker, the member who rented out the gym we played in, converted his two-car garage into an apartment and I moved in there. I didn't have to take the bus to work anymore. Instead, I rode to the club on my ten-speed bike. My alarm would go off at 5:30 in the morning and I'd be on my way. It was a beautiful, invigorating trip in the pre-dawn hours and I arrived at the club well ahead of the 6:20 draw. I was working seven days a week. It was not just the money that motivated me, it was the sense of not wanting to miss an opportunity. Every day I thought it might be the day when the right connection comes my way, the producer who will turn my life into a movie. I felt as if I were holding a winning lottery ticket but the numbers had not come up yet. I knew they would, maybe in a month or two months or a year, and I didn't want to take a chance that I wouldn't be there when they hit. So I didn't want to miss a single day.

One morning in June, I had one of my regulars ready to tee off on the tenth hole when the group grew to a foursome. The other three were Jeff Wilson of Wilson's Suede & Leather, the actor Ken Howard (of *White Shadow* fame), and a fellow by the name of Jim Cody, who would eventually help me open the last door on the way to my goal. Cody's wife was Jill Mazursky Cody, whose father Paul was (and is) a big Hollywood director/screenwriter/ actor; and she had solid movie credentials of her own. Among other credits, Jill had written the script for a film called *Gone Fishin'*, starring Joe Pesci and Danny Glover. I carried the bags for all four of them, which may have been a world record for caddies, and Cody, who had a good sense of humor, started calling me Super Caddy.

I was putting in an enormous number of hours per week, and the routine was beginning to wear me down. I had worked twenty-two straight days when the need for a day off asserted itself. The alarm went off about an hour before the dawn of a hot July day and I just didn't feel like working; I was totally exhausted. But there was something inside me that urged me to get out of bed and get to the club. I stayed in bed a while longer, but the voice that I had heeded all my life went from a whisper to a shout, yelling "You need to get to the Riviera today." It was 5:50 before I got myself going. I pedaled as fast as I could, but I got to the club late and missed the morning draw. There were more than twenty guys ahead of me and I was in no mood to spend the day waiting for something like the twenty-third job. So I was debating whether to stay or leave when Jim Cody came walking by the first tee. "Hey, Super Caddy," he said, "what's up?"

"You playing today?"

"Yeah," he said, "as a matter of fact, right now. We're the first off the tee at seven o'clock. You want to go?"

That invitation was as good as a request, and I was ready to go.

"I have a writer guy with me," Cody said. "You might want to talk with him."

The last time I'd caddied for Cody, about a month earlier, he had come up to me after the nine-hole round and said, "You're a little too sharp to be a caddy. What's your angle?" I told him about my treatment and, as it turned out, he had mentioned it to his writer friend. The writer was Dan Gilroy, a screenwriter who was also one of the best-paid script doctors in Hollywood. His credits included some major films, like *Freejack* and the Dennis Hopper–directed *Chasers*, and his talent apparently ran in his genes. His father was Frank D. Gilroy, whose play *The Subject Was Roses* won a Pulitzer Prize for drama and a Tony for best play in 1964; it was adapted for film four years later. Dan's brother Tony wrote the screenplays for the Jason Bourne trilogy and *The Devil's Advocate,* and he wrote and directed *Michael Clayton,* which was nominated for six Academy Awards, including best original screenplay. On top of it all, Dan was married to the actress Rene Russo. Clearly, I was in the right company. So was Dan Gilroy.

On the seventh hole, Dan was looking at a forty-five-foot birdie putt. I read the green and told him it was a two-foot break, right to left. He drilled it and became delirious. He was hugging me and we were high-fiving; he said it was the greatest shot he'd ever made, and he was a pretty good golfer who shot mostly in the low eighties. When the round was over, an appreciative Dan Gilroy told me that Cody had spoken to him about my treatment and that he would like to see it. A week later, while I was sitting in the caddy shack, my pager went off. It was Dan, inviting me to go to lunch. It was a two-hour lunch and, as I did with Richard

Reiner, I gave him my whole life story. We also talked about the world of sports gambling, and I learned that Dan liked staking a few bucks on football games during the season. Finally, we got around to my film treatment. Dan said he liked the thriller aspect of it, but it had been done before in one form or another.

"The real story here is your life," he told me. "That's something that hasn't been done before. Tell the story of how you became a sports handicapper, how you became who you are, why you walked away from it; describe the arc of rising to the top and then falling. I think you might have something here. Let me go home and talk to Rene about it. There are about five projects we're considering now. Let me see what she thinks of it, and I'll get back to you."

About a week later, the pay phone rang in the caddy shack. The caddy who answered said, "Brandon, it's for you." It was Dan.

"I'm working on another project right now," Dan said. "I'm rewriting the *Superman Lives* script and I'll be tied up for about six months. But I want to do a movie of your life and I don't want you talking to anybody else about it. So I'm going to offer you a six-month option on your story and I'll give you some money to get exclusive rights."

I said, "Fine, just give me a thousand bucks for the six months."

He said, "No, I'll do better than that. I'll give you three thousand for the six months."

I didn't even work that day. I felt that my lottery numbers had come in. I knew we would get this done; I knew it would happen. I didn't know how long it was going to take, but I had a respected screenwriter, from a respected family of screenwriters, and he was married to Rene Russo who might be right for a part in the picture. I couldn't do much better than that. Hollywood, here comes Brandon.

SLOUCHING TOWARD HOLLYWOOD

The first thing I learned about the movie business was that the wheels of the film industry grind even slower than the wheels of justice. In the summer of 1997, when I entered the deal with Gilroy, I had no idea that eight years would pass before the story of my life would find its way to the silver screen. Some of the pieces were in place right from the start; I had a well respected screenwriter who was married to a well respected actress who was eager for a part in the film. But that was just the beginning. There was the matter of lead actors to play me and Walter, the need for a director and a producer, and I was about to discover how mind-bending it was to put such a package together.

In the meantime, I decided it was time to take a leave of absence from the Riviera. It was the fall of 1997 and El Niño was forecast to bring a lot of rain to Southern California during the winter. I felt it would be a perfect time to take a little vacation in one of my favorite locations: Orlando, Florida. I called my best friend, Tommy O'Connell, who was hiring the staff for a new bar called the Roxy, which was to open in November. They needed a door manager and Tom said the job was mine for the asking and I took him up on his offer. Tommy was the head bartender, I was the door manager, and no two jobs could have suited us more. The club had its grand opening on November 7, and it was a smash hit. It was one of the first clubs in Orlando to strictly enforce the dress code that existed in some exclusive spots in cities like New York and Los Angeles.

Ten years ago, Orlando was still pretty much a hick town, and as the door manager of the Roxy I was someone to be reckoned with. I would stand at the door and decide who got in and who waited. If someone didn't look right to me, I would walk up and tell them that shirts without collars weren't allowed in tonight or maybe it would be no soft-soled shoes. It didn't matter what excuse I came up with; it was my job to put only the best-dressed people in the club. Of course the best-looking people were not always the best dressed, so looks often trumped attire. If

I spotted some hot-looking chicks in the middle of the pack I felt it my duty to grease the wheels. I would walk up the line and say, "Ladies, please come with me." I would lead them up the bar and tell Tommy to comp their drinks all night, and when the bar closed, Tom and I more often than not would be invited back to spend the night at their place.

While in Orlando, I got to meet my all-time favorite sports idol, Dr. J., Julius Erving. I also met the golf pro Ted Tryba, whom I later caddied for at the Riviera, and other notables and some not-so-notables. I was known in all the right places in town. Whether it was at Planet Hollywood, the Hard Rock Hotel, or any of the major golf courses, I was welcomed with a nod and a smile. I played golf for free, ate for free, and had all the gorgeous women I could handle. But it lasted just a few months. In February I got a call from Dan Gilroy. He was about to start work on the screenplay and he needed me back in L.A.

It was with mixed feelings that I left. True, I was moving closer to fulfilling my dream of making a movie of my life, but more immediately I was abandoning my role as Playboy of the Western World to schlep bags around a golf course. But there was no room for contemplation; I had to go. I checked out the relic of a car I had driven from California to Florida four months earlier and it still looked to be good for the trip. The car was a silver 1980 Mazda GLC two-door hatchback with about 250,000 miles on it. I had purchased it for $800 from a caddy by the name of Steve Hanamoto, who worked with me at the Riviera. Steve seemed to always have a car to sell and he became known at the club as Hanamoto Motors. But this one was particularly high risk. It was old enough to be an antique, and Hanamoto himself was afraid to drive it for twenty minutes into the valley. But I took a chance on it. I drove it to Las Vegas, had a mechanic look it over, and he said it would get me to Florida. It did. O'Connell christened it the Silver Bullet, a name derived from the beat-up cars Patrick Swayze drove in the 1989 film *Roadhouse*, in which he played a bouncer at a seedy roadside bar. Still, it had enough left in it to make the trip back to California, where I sold it to another caddy for $500. At a net cost of $300 for four months, the Silver Bullet had served me well.

At my first meeting with Dan I could feel the excitement beginning to build. We met in his office and then went to lunch with Rene. It was hard not to fall in love with her immediately and with both of them as a couple. They appeared to understand the difficulty a newcomer might have adjusting to the rhythms of Hollywood. They kind of adopted me and from that point on guided my entire experience in putting together the film. We never had a written contract. The whole deal was closed on a handshake. We devoted that first meeting to developing a pitch for the movie. We needed to attract top acting talent as well as a producer and director. All the while I was describing Walter to Dan, he kept saying that it would be a perfect vehicle for Dustin Hoffman. He described Dustin's quirks and hang-ups and it was like he was describing

Walter. Dustin had always been one of my favorite actors and the matchup seemed to be made to order. We decided to pitch it to him, and Dan said, "Dustin will either like you or hate you when he first meets you and that first reaction will never change. There is no in-between with him." I said, "Don't worry about it; he'll love me on sight." "How can you be so sure?" Dan asked. "Because," I said, "Walter loved me from the start, and if Dustin is that much like Walter, it's a sure thing."

We put the treatment together with Hoffman in mind. Rene had teamed with him in a 1995 film called *Outbreak* in which they played a couple in a broken marriage, and they were magic together. She said she had been hoping to do another movie with him. Putting them back together was going to be special. All we needed was for Hoffman to embrace the part of Walter and we would be on our way. My first visit to his office remains as vivid to me as if I were there right now. Rene and Dan were sitting on a couch in the middle of the office. Dustin was at his desk to the left of Rene, and I was directly across from Dustin to Dan's right. Dustin's glasses were perched at the edge of his nose and he was peering over the top looking at Dan and Rene, but he appeared to be totally distracted. He had some kind of art book in front of him and he was cutting pictures out of the book, toward what end I still don't know. Then he began fidgeting with something else and all the while Dan is pitching the film. Dustin would occasionally say something and then return to whatever else he was doing. At one point, Dan and Rene began discussing the particulars of her part, and I noticed Dustin looking right at me but not saying anything. It was a strained situation, and I decided to open things up a bit. I said, "I've heard you like to play tennis. Is that right?"

"Why?" he said. "Do you play?"

I said, "Didn't your mother ever teach you not to answer a question with a question?"

He laughed and said, "Yeah, I play tennis. Let me tell you something. I work out every morning with my tennis pro from Wimbledon. I have a clay court right in back of my house, and I hit two hundred serves every day." Then he got up, came around his desk, and walked right up to me. He pulled up his sleeve and displayed a fairly muscular forearm. "That's from the two hundred serves," he said. "I have a great serve." Next, he pulled up his pant leg and set his foot on my chair and said, "Look at this calf. That's from running up and down the court with my pro for about two and a half hours every morning."

I said, "Great! When are we going to play tennis?"

"When do you want to play?" he said.

I said, "You name the time and the place and we're playing."

"You got game?" he said.

"I think I got enough game for you," I said.

"I beat Agassi on my court," he warned me.

"You beat Agassi?"

Well, as it turned out, he came close; he won a point or two.

Now, we were all laughing and the atmosphere in the room had lightened up and Dustin seemed ready to do business. He picked up the phone and called his producer, Jay Cohen, and asked him to sit in on the rest of the meeting. Cohen, who was running Punch Productions at the time, was a young guy, probably about five years younger than me, and he eventually would play a major role in getting the picture made. Whether it was his interest in the project that made the difference, I couldn't tell, but Dustin suddenly had become enthusiastic. He had recently begun betting on pro football games and he loved the idea of playing a professional handicapper. "I love this role," he said. "This is me. This might be my next Academy Award. I'm ready to go, let's get going." Leaving his office, I felt that the pitch could not have gone better.

"It was great meeting you," I told him. "Now when are we going to play tennis?"

"What are you doing this weekend?" he asked me.

"Nothing," I told him.

"I'll have my secretary, Shelly, call you," he said.

That was on Thursday. On Friday morning, Shelly called and we set a date for Sunday morning at eight, at Dustin's house. When I moved back to L. A. I had rented a room in Tammy Chase's condo. It was Tammy who had introduced me to Richard Reiner and so, in a way, I had come full circle. I borrowed Tammy's VW and arrived promptly at eight. Dustin was waiting along with his tennis pro and Michael Ovitz, the former talent agent and Hollywood powerhouse. Ovitz had been the head of Creative Artists Agency from 1975 to 1995, when he left to become president of Walt Disney Co. under Chairman Michael Eisner. We played doubles and what I remember most is that Ovitz could not return my serve and he was getting kind of testy. But Dustin, now in his fifties, had a great tennis game. He could really play and I could barely believe that I was here playing tennis with Dustin Hoffman on his private clay court in back of his house. It was surreal. The song from *The Graduate* was playing in my head and I could see him in his sports car chasing Katherine Ross, and then I was seeing him in *Rain Man* and it also entered my consciousness that his tennis partner was arguably the most powerful man in Hollywood and I was driving tennis balls past him and enjoying every minute of it.

When we finished playing, Dustin told Ovitz he was going to do the movie and he had me do my pitch for him. During the next few weeks, as I spent a good deal of time with Dustin, he had me do my pitch for about twenty different people. He loved it. But for reasons I never understood, we were making no progress. Punch had optioned my life rights for a year, so I was locked in. Dan was writing the script and I was going to his office regularly and relating the story of my life to a tape recorder, but we couldn't get Dustin to commit. He kept saying he wanted to do the movie but he wouldn't sign on. We wanted him on board so we could go to a director and tell him that Dustin Hoffman was going to play a lead role. That would allow the director to offer some input as

Dan wrote the script. But it didn't happen. It just seemed that Dustin, who had taken a break from acting, was not yet ready to go back to work.

So we decided to approach it from the other end and set out to find a director. We went to Jon Avnet whose credits included *Up Close and Personal,* with Robert Redford and Michelle Pfeiffer. He seemed interested, but it didn't work out, and it began to occur to me that some sort of a miracle was necessary to get a picture made in Hollywood. You get into a situation where the actor you want doesn't like working with the director who is already committed to doing your project. So you either have to lose the actor or lose the director. You drop the director because you really want the actor and while the actor is waiting for the script to get done he takes on another project and makes a commitment to do something after that, so you lose him for three years. Now you have no director and no actor. So you start all over and go, say, to Jack Nicholson. His agent tells you he's not reading right now and if you want Jack to read the script, you'll have to wait for him. Now, if you give the script to Michael Douglas and Nicholson finds out that you didn't wait for him, he gets ticked off and tells you to get lost, and the whole cycle goes around again and again. So when people ask me why it took eight years to make this movie, that's the explanation they get.

In the meantime, Dan was busy writing the script and Dustin, who held a one-year option on the story, was playing the reluctant bride. He wouldn't commit to it and he wouldn't let it go, either. An amusing sidelight is that, after our first meeting in Dustin's office, I had a photo taken of me sitting on the couch with my left arm around Dustin and my right arm around Rene. Dustin was so enthusiastic and confident at the time, that he had written a dollar sign on a large white piece of paper and he and Rene held it right underneath my chin. The next day, I made a ton of copies of the photo and sent a mass mailing to just about everyone I knew, telling them the movie was on its way. It looked like a sure thing then, but that was before I knew anything about the mechanics of the Hollywood system. I did not have the slightest suspicion that eight tough years lay ahead of me.

In the final analysis, it was Jay Cohen who greased the wheels and got things moving. The first thing he did was get me out of my contract with Punch. Jay was running the production company for Dustin, but he felt the string was running out for them. He brought project after project to Dustin's attention and whether he liked them or not Dustin refused to make a commitment on any of them. Jay decided it was time to go in another direction, so he left Punch and went to work for a production company run by Kurt Russell and Goldie Hawn. While Dan was finishing the script, Jay was looking for a director, and I was back running the Riviera with Mike Cruz, making unheard of money for a country club caddy and enjoying my life in Southern California.

I kept in regular touch with Jay, who never let up. His office at Kurt and Goldie's production company was one street above the Riviera and I often went straight there after caddying. I would hang out in the office for a while and just blended into the scene. One way or the other, Jay and I remained connected. If I became discouraged, Jay would always pick me up. We had a routine going, where I would call and say, "Jay, four gunmen break into your house and they're holding your mother hostage. On your mother's life, are we making this movie?" He would never hesitate. "Yes," he'd say, "of course." Every now and then, I would up the ante. "Three Iranian gunmen have their guns pointed at your mother's head; her life depends on your answer . . ." "Yes, we're making the movie." He never wavered and never stopped working. Dan completed the script in 2000 and it would be another three years before we found a buyer for it. I did a lot of caddying in those three years and some of it was more than rewarding.

CADDY TO THE STARS

Being one of the top three caddies at the Riviera did not come without its privileges. I got paired up with most of the big names who came through, and they came from every echelon of every field and occupation, each aglitter with their own touch of stardom—athletes, actors, writers, producers. But none was bigger than the one I got on a bright spring day in 1999. I was hanging out in the caddy shack, playing cards, when a phone call came and the voice at the other end said, "Come on up, Brandon, you have the president."

President Bill Clinton was getting ready to play and he did not come unattended. As I walked up the hill to the first tee box, I turned the corner and saw twenty to twenty-five Secret Service agents in full camouflage gear all around the tee box. Some were carrying weapons, including full, big-scope M-16 rifles. It looked like they were preparing for war. They had every foot of the area surrounded and open sight lines in every direction. No one could have gotten within shouting distance of the president that morning; except for me and none of them bothered to find out who the hell I was. Wearing my white caddy uniform, I walked right up to the president of the United States and no one ever stopped me or questioned me. They never did a background check, they did not know my social security number, they did not know who I was or where I came from, I was never patted down or asked my name.

I walked right up to the president, stuck out my hand and said, "Mr. President, I'm Brandon Lang; I'm your caddy today and I'm looking forward to having a great day with you, sir." He turned to me with that big grin of his and in his Arkansas drawl he said, "Let's have some fun today, Brandon." And we did. He stepped up to the first tee and I said, "Just give me a little drive right down there in the middle of the fairway and maybe we can get you a birdie right here on number one." And all the while I was thinking, if you wanted to plot to assassinate the president, your best move would be to infiltrate a golf club where he played and wait until he showed up.

Aside from the trappings, caddying for Clinton was an experience in itself. He had some ability. You could see that he made a good turn on the ball and he hit it pretty solid. But he had an edge most players could only dream about. He carried three balls in his pocket and if he didn't like his first shot, he would drop a new ball and try again. If that one wasn't so good, he would go with a third ball.

Typically, I would say, "Mr. President, it's about 155 to the green; I think a nice little seven iron will do the job for you here, sir." He would take my advice, but if the ball hooked or sliced off course, he would just grin, drop another ball, and try again. Of course this practice created problems for the caddy, but I was not about to tell the president of the United States that he could not take a mulligan.

The result was that I ran my tail off that day. If I was near the green and he was 160 yards away and he chunked or shanked his first ball and it went to the left, then hooked the next one to the right, I had to leave the green, run back down the fairway, get the ball he hit to the left, swing back and run to get the other ball he hit to the right, then get up to the green with his putter and his ball cleaned, washed and ready to go before he made it to the green. I must have run the equivalent of two marathons that day and sweated away ten pounds chasing around for Three-Ball Billy. Scoring was also an adventure. On one hole, he had me put down a par, but it took him about eight strokes to get it because he used all three balls. But so far as I was concerned, he could bogey, double bogey or quadruple bogey, and if he said he had a par it was a par. I was caddying for the most powerful man in the world and I wasn't going to argue with him about his golf score. He was playing with three other guys who were unknown to me, and if they didn't protest, I certainly wouldn't say a word.

There were other complications as well. The Secret Servicemen seemed to be everywhere all the time. I was standing in the first fairway waiting for Clinton to hit when four golf carts drove by me with two agents in each cart. The first cart stopped ten feet away from me; the second stopped right behind the first green; the third went to the number two tee box and the fourth stopped in the middle of the number two fairway. It was a convoy of Secret Service people and they were constantly on the move. When the president was done on the fairway, the cart that was on the fairway went up to the green, the cart from the green went to the next tee box, and the cart from the tee box went to the fairway. It was a regular rotation from tee box to fairway to green to the next tee box. It was enough to drive you crazy, and Secret Servicemen would not be your first choice to make idle conversation with. They were as expressionless as faces on a totem pole.

I went up to two of them on the first green, waiting for Three-Ball Billy to hit, and said, "What's up?" They looked at me as if I were the suspect in a capital crime. They made no response; they just looked me straight in the eye and turned away. At that point I decided that before the round was over I wanted to make one of those guys smile. There was a television show in the sixties and seventies (revived in the late nineties) called *Make Me Laugh*, where three comics would come out on stage and each would be given a minute to make a contestant laugh. I thought I was a pretty funny guy and I had more than a minute and I was determined to make one of them show his teeth. One of two things was going to happen before the day was over: either Brandon Lang was going to be taken into custody and booked on one or another federal charge or he was going to get a laugh from a member of the Secret Service.

When we got to the sixth hole, a par three, the same two guys were up near the green who had stared me down at the first hole. I walked up to them and said, "Come on, man, give me something on the guy. I swear I'll never repeat it. But let's be honest. If I'm the president of the United States, I might have some Playmates or Penthouse pets stored in an underground passage or somewhere, if I were inclined in that direction, but Monica Lewinsky? That's embarrassing, man." Neither one of them so much as curled a lip. With that, the first player put a ball on the green and I took my second shot at them. "Come on, guys, let something slip," I said. "You must have plenty of stories to tell. Look, Kennedy screwed around, but he had Marilyn Monroe. *Marilyn Monroe!* Are you going to tell me the best Billy could do was *Monica Lewinsky?*" I almost had them with that. I could see them trying to suppress a smile. I doubt that any caddy had toyed with them this way before and they were not going to give in easily.

It crossed my mind that if the agents didn't take what I was doing in the right spirit, they might try to make some trouble for me with management; this guy Brandon is playing fast and loose with the U.S. Secret Service; he's showing disrespect for the president. But I didn't think I had much to worry about. The round with the president was not long after the 1999 Nissan Open, in which I caddied for Ted Tryba and he set the course record by shooting 61 on Saturday. Ernie Els went on to win the tournament while Ted finished in a second-place tie with Tiger Woods and Davis Love III. No PGA tour caddy owns the course record with a player at the Riviera; it's a Riviera caddy with a PGA tour player who holds the record, so I felt pretty secure.

Five holes later came a long par five, so I had some time walking out on the eleventh fairway and one of the agents comes up to me and says, "What's your story?"

"What do you mean?"

He says, "Give me your social security number; I want to check you out."

I could tell from his manner that he was just having some fun with me, so I said, "Are you nuts? You'll put my number in a high-tech computer and have me arrested on some trumped up charge on my drive home tonight. The next thing I know, you'll have me in jail, buried deep in some prison in Turkey, never to be heard from again. Forget that, man, I know all about Turkish prisons and I ain't ready for that because I like my ass." With that came chuckles from both, their teeth flashing white. On the next hole, when I approached their cart, one of them said, "We've watched a lot of caddies along the way, but you're the first of your kind. You know what? I do have a story for you but I don't think you're ready for it yet."

Two holes later, I walked up to them and started chatting and they both gave me their cards and said, "Anytime you're in D.C. give us a call and we'll show you around and maybe tell you a story or two." They had never been to L.A. before and I gave them the name of a sushi place and my phone number. That night they called and told me it was the best sushi they ever had. One of my few lingering regrets is that I never got to D.C. and missed out on the chance to hang out with a couple of Secret Service agents.

It was the eighteenth hole that capped the day. Clinton had a very makeable ten-foot bogey putt; a legitimate bogey on 18 at Riviera was pretty impressive, and he really wanted to make it as a way to crown his day. He bent down behind the ball, and you have to remember all the agents who were spread out across the course on the earlier holes were now all gathered around the eighteenth green watching. Including the other players and the head pro, there must have been twenty-five people there, and you could see that Clinton had a real desire to sink the putt. As he was leaning over, sizing up the shot, I leaned down next to him and whispered, "Mr. President, before I give you this read, I just have to know . . . What were you thinking?" He took off his hat and put it down to his chest and started chuckling. At that point, I put my hand on his shoulder and said, "Inside left firm and don't be short," and turned away. He looked at me as I walked away and I winked at him and watched him drain the putt. All told, it was a good day. He clocked out in the high 80s, but even if he hadn't used two or three balls here and there, he probably would have been between 95 and 100, which is not a bad score at the Riviera.

Once you've caddied for the president of the United States, most other assignments pale in comparison, but there were a number of lesser celebrities that I loved working with who gave me some memorable days. Tom Cruise was one of the best. Tom and Nicole Kidman, his wife at the time, were both tennis members. They were clients of Buster McCoy, the number one tennis pro, who gave them lessons regularly and I had a special relationship with Buster. Buster pretty much subsidized me when I was working with him. I was new at the club at that time and I was struggling to make my monthly $400 rent payments. Buster always tided me over. I referred to him as the Bank of Buster, where I could always go for a loan. He was also available to meet other needs, such as a hot dinner on occasion, and he tipped me off whenever one of his tennis celebrities was booked for a round of golf.

One Monday he told me that Tom Cruise would be playing the following day at 1:30. I looked at the starter sheet and saw the name Tom Cruise and next to it the letters RTC—Riviera Tennis Club. Tennis members were entitled to play two rounds of golf a year, and if Cruise was coming I wanted to carry his clubs. I went to Mike Cruz, but he wasn't going to be working that day. I spoke with Glen in the pro shop and he said he would see what he could do. But I didn't want to leave it to chance. I decided to play a long shot. On Tuesday morning I called Dustin Hoffman and got his secretary, Shelly, on the phone. I said, "Shelly, can you do me a favor? Can you have Dustin call Tom Cruise and ask him to request me when he comes to play golf this afternoon?" I don't know whether she ever called Dustin or Dustin called Cruise, but that afternoon the phone rang in the caddy shack and Glen said, "Come on up, you've got Tom Cruise. And you better hurry because his assistant called and said he's running late. You need to pick him up in the parking lot."

I raced up to the top, got in the cart, and waited in the parking lot. Then, here he comes. Tom Cruise pulls up in his Porsche, top down, and apologizes for being late. I grab his clubs from his trunk and I see he is toting a brand new set of Callaway irons that look like they've never struck a golf ball. "Have you ever played with these?" I ask him.

He says, "I've only played golf twice in my life."

"And you're coming out here to play the Riviera?"

"Why not?" he says. "I always wanted to play here."

"This really is a tough course to play when you're learning," I tell him.

But he's as cool as can be. "We'll figure it out," he says.

We get to the first tee, where his mom and dad are waiting along with a dozen other people hovering about to see Tom Cruise hit a golf ball, and I can see how nervous he is. I knew from experience that when a player is nervous he is likely to hit over the top of the ball on the first tee. So I tell Tom to just try to make solid contact. Don't try to drive the ball deep; just hit it squarely. You don't want to dribble it off the tee. I tell him to tee the ball up extra high and close the club face towards him. He follows my instructions explicitly, swings smoothly, and sends the ball 220 yards down the middle of the fairway. Then he turns and looks at me, and I throw my arms out, palms up, as if to say, "What else would you expect?"

He's as happy as a little kid on Christmas morning. "That's the best drive I've ever hit in my life," he says.

"Calm down," I tell him. "We have a long way to go, buddy, and we'll have a lot of bad shots and a few good ones."

He's hitting the ball pretty well and having a good time, but when we get to the third hole, a par four, he slices it to the right and into the rough. He has about 125 yards for his third shot and there's a big bunker in front of the hole. When I caddied for celebrities who didn't play very often I helped them out of tight spots as much as I could. When the ball is deep in the rough, as Tom's was, I'd lift it out and by the time they'd get there it'd be in the same spot but sitting right on top. The rough at the Riviera is as unforgiving as barbed wire. If you let your club get down into it, it will just grab hold of the head and you won't be able to get it out. So when Tom gets to his ball he has a perfect lie right on top of the rough. Still, he will have to pick the ball clean to get onto or near the green.

I take out a six iron, which is not what you would normally use from 125 yards, and Tom seems to have his doubts. I tell him, "Look, I want you to do exactly what I tell you, and if you do you might pull off a miracle shot. I want you to take the six iron halfway back on your swing and when you come down to hit the ball, I want you to tell yourself that it's not grass beneath the ball; it's cement and ice and you can't let your club hit it. You must skim the ball right off the top and as soon as you make contact I want you to stop your swing and see what happens."

What I want him to do is to hit a little punch cut with that six iron, carry over that bunker onto the green and get himself a par four. The odds against him pulling that off are more than I would care to calculate, but actors have something special that they bring to the table. They know how to follow directions and they are able to mimic what they see and hear. And Tom was about to prove my point. He brings his club halfway back, just as I told him, comes down clean, and stops his club. But he catches the slightest bit of the grass and hits it a little fat. It looks like it's heading into the bunker, but it lands on the grass, on the face of the bunker, and rolls onto the green, six feet from the cup. Tom can't control himself. He drops his club and leaps into my arms, like the famous photo of Yogi Berra wrapping himself around Don Larsen after he pitched his perfect game in the 1956 World Series. It was the greatest shot he ever hit, but he soon learned how humbling a game golf can be. He left his par putt just a few inches short of the cup.

By the time we got to the seventh hole we were chatting like old buddies. I was sitting in the cart and I asked him, "Did you get a call from Dustin Hoffman today?" He looked a bit puzzled. I'm just a caddy at the Riviera; how would I know that Dustin Hoffman called him?

"Yeah," he said, "he left a message but I didn't get a chance to call him back."

"I can tell you what the message was," I said. "I had called him to ask you to request me as your caddy."

"How do you know Dustin?" he asked.

"Well," I said, sounding as casual as I could, "Dustin is going to play my boss in a movie about my life." I proceeded to fill in the details and he says, "That's a great story." Then I told him, "I thought Dustin would be great as my boss and that you would be perfect to play me. It would be nice to reunite you two guys again after *Rain Man*. But Dustin thought you were a little too old to play me."

Actually, Tom and I are about the same age, and he took umbrage. "Too old?" he said. "What does he mean too old? Too old for what? Why am I too old?"

"I don't think you're too old," I said. "I think you'd be perfect."

"It's unbelievable he would say that," he said.

Tom had time for only nine holes, but his mom and stepdad stayed on for the back nine. Three hours later, on my way home, I got a call from Jay Cohen.

"What did you say to Tom Cruise that got him so upset?" he asked me.

"Nothing," I said. "I just told him that I thought he would be perfect to play me in the movie and bring him and Dustin together again, but that Dustin said he was too old. Why do you ask?"

"Because twenty minutes after he left the golf course he called Dustin and asked why Dustin said he looked too old. Isn't that hilarious?"

"Well," I said, "I don't think he was too offended because after nine holes he slipped me a hundred dollars, and his mom and stepdad each gave me a hundred at the end of the round. So all told, I got three hundred dollars for having a great day with *Top Gun* Tom Cruise."

I thought it was curious how Tom—who oozed confidence in everything he did—could be so insecure about his age. I guess age is the demon that haunts actors because it dictates what roles might be available to them. One actor who betrayed no insecurity whatever was Jack Nicholson. Jack was, to quote the title of one of his movies, as good as it gets. I got the loop to caddy for him through Rudy Durand, a screenwriter and director and a long-time member of the Riviera. Rudy was kind of an all-purpose factotum who seemed to have a finger in every pie but never his own full slice. He knew almost everyone, but not as well as he made it seem, and my general feeling was that he often promised more than he delivered. Well, it was Rudy who hooked me up with Nicholson, but it was not a direct connection.

BEATING THE ODDS

I was the regular caddy for a Japanese billionaire by the name of Peter Lam, who was one of the richest men in Japan. He gambled so big on the course that he had a personal accountant who followed him in a cart and kept track of the bets, which could run as high as $25,000 or $30,000 a hole. One day Peter came out for a practice round a day before a big-money match with some other Japanese bigwigs and Rudy was out there with him. Also with him was his personal golf pro, an American by the name of Brad, who would sometimes offer bits of advice, maybe adjusting his swing, but Peter trusted me completely when it came to selecting clubs. At one point, Brad came up to me and said, "Of all the courses Peter plays, including the one at his own club, he never lets anyone tell him what to hit. You're the only one he allows to club him." Rudy heard this and was very impressed.

When the round was over, Rudy said to me, "I'm bringing Jack Nicholson up here on Saturday, and I want you to caddy for us." I gave him my card but I never heard from him. I knew well enough that you couldn't always take what Rudy said literally, but he did have a connection with Nicholson. They co-sponsored the Jack Nicholson–Rudy Durand Celebrity Golf Classic, so it was not a stretch to think he would bring Nicholson out to play. Saturday came and went with no sign of Rudy or Jack. But on Sunday morning, as I'm about to finish my round and go home, I see Jack and Rudy on the practice green. I walk up to Rudy and say, "Thanks for letting me know."

He said he lost my card, but it wasn't too late. "Caddy for us now," he says, and I accept the invitation.

Caddying for Jack was like caddying for the Joker, like caddying for McMurphy, the character he played in *One Flew over the Cuckoo's Nest*. I had the same feeling of disbelief that I had playing tennis with Dustin Hoffman. How did a guy like me get to rub shoulders with two of Hollywood's biggest stars? Jack was no different from what you expected after seeing his movies. He had that same high-eyebrowed quizzical look when he found himself in a spot he couldn't get out of, the same demonical laugh when it suited the occasion. He also had some peculiarities that I had never encountered before. On the second hole I made a really bad read on a putt. I told him I didn't have his yardage exactly right on number one either. When we got to number three, I noticed that there were two dots on the scorecard. "What are those dots for?" I asked him.

"Those are caddy errors," he said, "they're not player errors. It's not my fault that you misread the putt, it's not my fault you didn't get the yardage right on number one. So what I do is, when I'm done with my round, whatever score I have, I subtract all the caddy errors and that's my real score. That's what I would have shot if you got it right." "What kind of shit is that?" I said. "I never heard of taking points off for caddy errors." But that was typical Jack Nicholson and I had to laugh about it.

From that point on, I was spot-on for the rest of the day. My yardage estimates were right, my reads were on the money. When we got to the eleventh hole, Jack was 119 yards to the flag and there was a big bunker on the right-hand side. Jack says, "How far?"

I say, "It's 119 yards with a little bit of wind in our face, and it plays uphill, so here's a nine iron."

"No," he says, "I use my pitching wedge up to 120."

I say, "Jack, it's a nine iron."

"Not for me," he says. "I hit my pitching wedge to 120."

"Okay," I say, "here's your pitching wedge. Now I'm going to stand in the bunker because that's where you're going to hit it." And he does.

As he's walking to the bunker I take the ball out of my pocket and say, "Here, give me the wedge." I take the wedge and hand him his nine iron, hand him a ball and say, "Now go back and try it with the nine. Humor me, would you please?" He walks back to the fairway, drops the ball, and puts it right up on the green. Now, he walks to the bunker, picks out a sand wedge, puts the ball onto the green and starts to walk away.

"Where are you going?" I ask him. "You hit it in the bunker because you didn't listen to me. That's a player error, not a caddy error, and I don't rake bunkers when it's a player error, so you rake it." With that, I toss the rake at Jack's feet, and Rudy is doubled over with laughter. And before long, Jack is laughing almost as hard.

After that, it's smooth sailing through to the eighteenth hole, where Jack needs a fifteen-foot putt for par. Eighteen is a tough hole at the Riviera and Jack says, "I've got to make this one; what's it going to do?"

"You want the truth?" I ask him.

He nods and I shoot back at him one of his most famous lines, from the movie *A Few Good Men*: "You can't handle the truth." It is the perfect line to ease the pressure of the moment. Jack loves it and as he goes to line up the putt, I give him the read. "It's uphill so you have to try to hit it a foot past the hole on the left edge."

He turns and looks at me and asks, "Are you sure?"

I look over at Rudy and say, "Am I sure? Have I missed a read since the third hole?"

"No, you haven't," he says.

I turn back to Jack and say, "It's left edge firm."

Jack sinks the putt, makes his par, and I pick up a cool two hundred bucks for hanging with the Joker.

SKIMMING THE CREAM— GRETZKY, JORDAN, WOODS

Not surprisingly, athletes tended to be even more competitive than actors on the golf course, but they were every bit as different in their approach and their attitude toward the game. I had the opportunity to caddy for two athletes who were widely considered to be the best there ever were in their sports—Wayne Gretzky in hockey and Michael Jordan in basketball—and the contrast between them could not have been greater. To me, they were like bookends that sealed the range from best to worst. Gretzky was one of the nicest people I have ever been around, humble, gracious, accommodating. In my opinion, Jordan possessed none of those attributes. He acted as if the whole world revolved around him, that he was better than me because of who he was.

I had heard about what a good guy Gretzky was before I got to caddy for him back in 2001. He was a member of the Sherwood Country Club in L.A., and I was told that he once took a couple of the caddies on a two-day sabbatical down to Phoenix to watch one of his hockey games. He had a really sweet personality. I asked him questions about anything and everything. He talked about his career and what it felt like to be retired. Did he miss the game? He told me he missed the players more than the game itself. You form a close alliance with your teammates over the course of the seasons; you come to rely on one another, and that kind of camaraderie is available only in certain situations and is nearly impossible to replace. We chatted as if we were old buddies, sharing our views and our sentiments.

He happened to be a pretty good golfer as well. He had a nice swing and a great putting stroke. He was playing with three friends of his and since no one won any of the first four holes, five skins were at stake on the fifth. Wayne had about a six-foot putt for par, which would have given him the hole and all five skins, and I gave him a bad read on the break. I thought it would break a little more than it did. I gave him a ball out on the right, and it should have been a ball inside the hole. He hit it exactly as I told him but the ball didn't break into the hole; it rolled right by the break.

Being as genuine and decent a guy as he is, Wayne said, "Throw the ball back here and let me try it again. I think I hit that a little too hard." He hit the next one really slow, inside the hole, and it dropped right in. "I knew I hit the first one too hard," he said. But he hadn't. He hit it exactly as I told him to, but he was trying to spare me the embarrassment of giving him a bad read. I took his putter from him and said, "Listen to me, I appreciate your trying to cover for me, but that was as bad a read as I made all day, and before the round is over I'll make it up to you." I winked and he smiled back at me, which was his way of saying that we understood each other. I can't remember another occasion where a player tried to take responsibility for my mistake. It showed me that Gretzky was really special.

The rest of the day was a breeze. I gave him some really good reads on several holes. On number twelve, I gave him great yardage—about 170 yards in, accounting for the slight wind coming at us. He wanted to use a six-iron and I told him to use the five. As I handed it to him I said, "And when you speak of me, speak well," and walked away laughing. He used the five, got within about ten feet of the hole, and made his birdie. On number sixteen, he had a birdie putt that he thought would break a little right to left, but I told him it was dead straight. He hit it that way and drained it. He thanked me and I thanked him for a great day. The member who was part of his foursome gave me $150 and Wayne gave me a $200 slider.

I didn't expect much from Jordan when I caddied for him because his reputation had preceded him. When I was working as door manager at the Roxy nightclub in Orlando, I got to know a little bit about how celebrities tip. The biggest tipper I ever met was Horace Grant of the Chicago Bulls. He would fold up a one hundred dollar bill as small as possible and press it into my hand when he walked into the club and he would do it again when he left. Years ago, *Sports Illustrated* ran an article on the best and worst tippers among professional athletes. Grant, Gretzky, and Mark Messier were among the ones at the top and Jordan was down near the bottom. So I had some idea about what awaited me when I went out to caddy for him. I learned not to even bother sucking up to him because no matter what I did I couldn't get a dime out of the man.

To paraphrase the old joke, he may be cheap but he makes up for it by being arrogant as well. I don't think Jordan was a bad player, but he was not nearly as good as he seemed to think he was. We rubbed each other the wrong way right from the start. I would give him great reads and he would argue with me about them or just ignore them. The Riviera was my club; it was my golf course and if you want to play it the correct way you'll take my advice; not many people knew the intricacies of the course better than I did. But Jordan showed no respect for my knowledge at all. It was also impossible to make small talk with him. He was the exact opposite of Gretzky in that regard. When I said something or asked him a question, he either looked away or glared at me, as if to say, "Who are you to be asking me questions?"

Despite not heeding my advice, Jordan hit some pretty great shots that day. He probably shot about 91, and I've seen PGA tour players shoot no better than 83 at the Riviera. If you're not accustomed to the course, the Riviera can bring really good players to their knees. There's no question that Jordan has some real talent. He is an unbelievable natural athlete who probably could excel at any sport he dedicated himself to. I have enormous respect for him as a basketball player, but, personally, I believe he leaves a lot to be desired as a person. I recall an interview he did with Ted Koppel on the old *Nightline* television program. Koppel was questioning Jordan about his lack of social activity. The Jordan brand sneakers sold at prices that few inner city kids could afford, and Jordan was nowhere to be heard from on issues of equality where his voice could have made a huge difference. Koppel asked him why he did not take political positions that could have a positive effect, perhaps raising the social consciousness of the African-American kids who idolized him. Jordan's response was brief and unfortunate: "Republicans buy sneakers too."

Tiger Woods, who is to golf what Jordan is to basketball and Gretzky is to hockey, has a reputation for being somewhat aloof, and people sometimes view him as being as detached from the public as Jordan is. It isn't true. Like many athletes or other public figures, Woods is protective of his privacy; he does not like being the center of attention unless he is on the golf course. He is not as openly friendly as Gretzky, but by no means is he as self-admiring as Jordan is.

I first met Tiger long before he was Tiger Woods. It was in 1984. I was in the navy and learning to play golf at the Los Alamitos Navy Course when I saw a small African-American kid come crawling underneath the fence to join his father on the third hole, a par three. The dad looked at me and my buddies and said, "Do you mind if my son jumps in and plays with me?"

"Absolutely not," I said. "Go ahead."

We watched the kid tee up the ball and drive it with as good a golf swing as I've ever seen. I walked over to the dad and said, "How old is your kid?"

"He's eight."

I looked him straight in the eye and said, "Tell me his name, because twelve years from now when he wins the Masters I'll be able to say I spotted this kid as a champion when he was eight years old."

The dad said, "I'm Earl Woods and this is my son, Tiger." We allowed them to play through.

Fifteen years later, in 1999, I convinced one of my closest friends, Ted Tryba, to let me caddy for him in the Nissan Open. That was when Ted shot the course-record 61, and we had a two-shot lead going into Sunday, when Ted was paired with Davis Love and Tiger Woods. On the first tee, Tiger actually came up to me and said, "Great job with Ted this week; good luck today."

I said, "Well, this isn't the first time I've met you. I met you when you were eight years old on the Los Alamitos course when I was in the navy. We met again under unusual circumstances in 1996, the year you won the Las Vegas Invitational. I woke up early Wednesday and watched you play your first round at the old Stardust course. You had shot a one-under and you weren't too happy about it. Later that evening, in a local club, I was taking a leak in the men's room when you walked in and a guy there was heckling you, wouldn't leave you alone, and the bouncer had to throw the guy out of the place. You were standing next to me and I said, 'Son, you're holding greatness in your hand, be gentle with it.'" Tiger started laughing. I tapped him on the shoulder, said "Good luck today," and walked away. An underage Tiger Woods had all the luck he needed. In the five-round tournament in Las Vegas, he went lights-out the last four rounds and won the first PGA title of his professional career.

It was not just casual politeness when Tiger congratulated me for the job I was doing with Ted. Caddies play a bigger role in a golfer's performance than most observers give them credit for. Ted had never come close to setting a course record with his regular caddie and this was the first time I was caddying for him, so maybe I accounted for part of the difference. Nobody in the tournament that weekend knew the course better than I did. By the same token, Tiger was having some troubles with his own caddy, Mike "Fluff" Cowan. Immediately after Sunday's final round he fired Fluff, and a few weeks later picked up Stevie Williams, who still caddies for him a decade later. Throughout the tournament, Tiger was as cordial and friendly as could be under extremely tense conditions. He has a reputation for being wary of strangers who might be looking to move in on him and lay claim to his attention, but when you are inside the ropes, you are a guest in his office and he will treat you with respect. All told, he carries himself with class and dignity.

He was already an international celebrity in 1999, and it was a far more mature Tiger Woods than the one I met three years earlier at the Las Vegas Invitational. Back then he was just twenty years old but he had about him the air of a man who knew that he owned part of the future. According to his trainer, Butch Harmon, however, he was as green as most any other twenty-year-old. I spoke with Butch, who started working with Tiger when he first turned pro and shared in some of Woods's early successes.

"It's hard to believe how naïve he is," Butch said. "He has no idea how much money he has now. The other day we pulled into a McDonald's, and he didn't have any money with him. I said, 'Tiger, you're a multi-millionaire, how can you not have any cash in your pocket?' He just shrugged and said, 'How am I going to pay for this?' Can you imagine what it would have been like if I hadn't been with him? Headline of the day: Tiger Woods can't pay for a McDonald's hamburger. He had no idea how much money he was worth."

As we were chatting, we saw Tiger walk by heading for the next hole. Butch shook his head and smiled. "We have only just begun to tap into the talent this kid has," he said, "and when I'm through with him he'll be the greatest we've ever seen."

14

ON HOLLYWOOD'S RED CARPET

All the while I was cavorting around the Riviera with celebrities of every stripe, Jay Cohen was shopping the movie script. He was trying to match actors who would be right for the parts with directors who were interested in making the film. At the start it seemed hopeless. If a director was interested, the actor of the moment didn't please him; if the actor seemed eager, he didn't want to work with this or that director. When one zigged, the other zagged, and so it went for several years.

Our first big bite was Ashton Kutcher, the star of the TV series *That 70s Show*, and perhaps better known as the youthful husband of actress Demi Moore. We met with him and two weeks later he called Gilroy and Cohen and made the surprising and somewhat incredible request that he have full control of the script, including what is known as the privilege of a page-one rewrite, meaning that he would be able to change anything in the script from page one forward. Jay and Dan said that no one was getting that kind of control over the script, and that ended our relations with Kutcher.

By 2002, I started to think that it was just not going to happen. It occurred to me that I might go back into handicapping; I was certain that being a professional handicapper would eventually be the call of my future, but in the meantime I was making a great living caddying and living the good life, so I was in no hurry to make a decision. But at the start of 2003, things finally began to fall into place for the film.

After a number of production companies turned down the script, Morgan Creek said they liked it and agreed to produce the movie. Rene Russo was the first member of the cast to come aboard. She told her agent she wanted to play the part of Walter's wife. Rene's agent also represented Al Pacino, so he gave the script to Pacino, who was a natural to play Walter. Both were happy with D. J. Caruso as director, and he was pleased with them. The part of Brandon Lang was yet to be filled. Among the first to throw his hat in the ring was a young actor by the name of Hayden Christensen, who had played Anakin Skywalker in the *Star Wars* prequels. He thought he was exactly right for the part and was so eager to play it that I flew to New York to watch him do a read with Pacino while Caruso was present. We met in a room at the Ritz-Carlton and you could see that Hayden was thrilled to be reading lines with Al Pacino. Listening to them read I fully appreciated what a great job Dan had done with the script; he nailed it exactly right. As for Hayden, I thought he did a credible job, but Al felt he was not old enough and not quite ready. I remember standing in the street with Hayden in the middle of New York City, seeing how high he was from just running lines with Al Pacino and it was right then that I first felt entirely confident that the picture would be made.

There also were rumors that Leonardo DiCaprio was interested in the part as well as Josh Hartnett, of *Black Hawk Down* fame, and Colin Farrell, a Golden Globe Award–winning Irish actor. I know that Josh read the script and so did the late Heath Ledger. For one reason or another, neither one connected. Finally, Jay gave the script to Matthew McConaughey, who was known to place a wager on a sporting event now and then, and he loved the idea of playing a sports handicapper. Now the whole team was in place, but one change still had to be made. My name in the script was Lane, but when we discovered that someone already was using the name Brandon Lane in a film script, we changed it to Lang.

It was at this time, with production of the movie just over the horizon, that I realized I would have to give up caddying. If the film was going to have the impact I wanted it to have, particularly in Hollywood circles, I could not have people thinking of me as a caddy in a white jump-suit rather than as a handicapper. With filming scheduled to start in September of 2004, I officially retired from the Riviera Country Club in June. I missed it more than I thought I would. I missed hanging around the caddy shack with the other guys, waiting for the morning draw, working the course with all sorts of interesting characters, the whole lifestyle, just living it day by day, loop by loop.

Making the movie was front-and-center now and no time was wasted in getting started. The whole process begins with what is called a table read. Everyone sits around a huge table and the script is read by the actors playing each part. In addition to the stars, a bunch of char-acter actors are brought in to read the secondary parts. In all, there were about twenty-five people sitting there reading the script aloud. I remember watching this unfold and feeling the energy that was produced. I was at the far end of the table with Pacino to my right and Rene to my left, along with an actor named Jeremy Sisto, who read McConaughey's part. Matt would be there for the second read. Next to Al were Dan, Jay Cohen, and Pacino's agent. I was on an emotional high, but what really choked me up was that my brother Bryan was there too.

Bryan had called me from Vegas and I filled him in on everything that was going on and he asked if he could come to the table read. Sitting there with my brother while my whole life, and much of his too, was unwinding for all the public to see, was like an out-of-body experience. Bryan and I looked at each other as episodes from our past were brought forth. It was as if we were pinching each other to make sure it was all real. I had embarked on a journey to make this happen in May of 1996. For eight years I had been telling people about it as if it were a sure thing, and after a while they began to doubt me. Now, here we were; it was happening and I could hardly believe it. I could tell by looking at Bryan that he was as moved as I was. Deep down, Bryan probably knew me better than anyone on the planet. He knew I had always been a dreamer and now he was there as my biggest dream was about to come true. It was as big a high as two kids from a small town in Michigan could have.

After the read, Bryan and I went to a sushi bar on Santa Monica Boulevard and, as if to put an exclamation point on the whole day's experience, we sat down at the bar and to our immediate left was Henry Winkler, the Fonz. To our right was Tori Spelling and her mother. Bryan looked left, then right, then at me and said, "This is unbelievable."

"Bryan," I told him, "this is what you see every day in this part of town. These people live here and they go out in public just like everybody else."

Then he smiled, put his arms around me, and said, "You did it, you really did it."

After the first read everyone made notes on what adjustments should be made, gave them to Dan, and he did a quick rewrite. We had a second read about two months later with pretty much the whole cast there. It was interesting watching McConaughey preparing to play me. He watched a number of my old Mike Anthony tapes and said he wanted to play me at a lower key. He didn't think the high-energy, Gatling-gun delivery would work for him. We didn't spend much time together. We had about three conversations; the longest lasted about twenty-five minutes. He asked me questions that he thought got to the heart of the character and he got it spot-on. He did a great job.

Filming began in September 2004, with release scheduled a year later. Most of the film was shot in Vancouver, with some of the scenes shot in Las Vegas and New York. The only filming sessions I attended were those in New York. I hung out a bit with Matt, who was basically a good ol' boy from Texas. We had some good times together but he was busy most of the day and I was spending most of my time with my future wife, Kim. Pacino kept pretty much to himself. He would just wait around, often sitting in his limousine until he was needed on the set. I had a small cameo part in the movie, filmed in New York City. Kim insists that my part should be called a "cam," not a cameo because I was not on screen long enough to get the "eo." After my brief part was shot, Kim and I stopped by Brooklyn and watched the filming of the scene in which Rene jumps into the Mercedes with Matt and takes off on a wild ride. Then I said goodbye to everyone and the next time I saw any of them was at the red carpet premiere.

The premiere of the film was the most incredible experience of my entire life. I took my mom and that's what made it so special. To appreciate the feeling, you have to understand where my mom came from and every-thing that happened to her throughout her life. I was the youngest of her children and her golden boy and given the hardscrabble existence during the early years of our lives, to think that here she was in L.A. at this unbelievable moment in her son's life was nothing short of staggering. I wanted to take her to Nordstrom's and get her a complete makeover for the big night, but she flatly refused to go to Beverly Hills. She thought it was too rich for her blood. There also was a Nordstrom's in the Westside Pavilion, just below Beverly Hills and I took her there to get her gussied up for the big night. I told the sales lady that she is going to the red carpet premiere tonight to see a movie about her son's life. I said, "Dress this woman up and make her look like royalty; price is no object." It was like the scene from the movie *Pretty Woman* in which the hotel manager, played by Hector Elizonda, tells the saleslady that Julia Roberts gets whatever she wants. My mom got the same treatment, and I must say that she looked spectacular. I had a hairdresser come to my place and a limo picked us up at the hotel. Bryan was there too, along with Kim, my publicist, and a number of my good friends.

We sipped champagne throughout the trip, and when the limo pulled up in front of the Academy of Motion Pictures and Arts there were photographers waiting there, ten to twelve deep, and they were saying, "Brandon, up here; Brandon look this way; right this way; big smile, Brandon." You have a smile fixed to your face so people can get the picture they want; you're like a bobblehead doll moving this way and that and then you move along. It had been arranged for me to get there about fifteen minutes before Al, Matt, and Rene, so that I could enjoy my moment of fame without competition, and after making the walk down the red carpet, when the photographers were done, there were the TV interviews to be conducted, one station after another, with my mom right behind me and I could see tears in her eyes and she reveled in the moment. I got emotional too. I almost broke down while I was being interviewed by KTLA, Channel 5. I had to ask them to give me a minute, and then I hugged my mom, I hugged her on TV, right at the end of the red carpet, and broke down crying. My whole life came rushing back, all the tough times in my childhood, the pain my mom was forced to suffer, and it all came down to this. It made no sense and defied reality. There are people walking the earth who have done more than I could ever dream of doing and here I was in the limelight. Why me? I kept thinking: What did I do to deserve this?

I loved the movie, and so did everyone else, and the reception afterward was wonderful. I met a whole world of celebrities and had my picture taken with many of them, including the champion tennis sisters, Serena and Venus Williams. I posed with Matt, with Matt and his mom, Matt and my mom, with Dan and Rene, and everyone else of note. The only photo I missed was one with Al. When I posed with him, my brother's camera went dead, and Al ducked out early so I never got another picture with him.

On Hollywood's Red Carpet

Two for the Money opened on October 6, 2005, to middling reviews and a weak showing at the box office. While it doesn't account for poor reviews, the weekend of October 6 had to be one of the worst times for a movie of this type to open, for it completely ignored its potential audience. Here was a movie about sports gambling and it opened on a weekend that features the opening of baseball's playoffs along with college football on Saturday and pro football on Sunday. As soon as I heard the release date, I called Dan and said, "You better use whatever influence you have to change the date because sports fans, especially those who bet on the games, are not going to the movies when they can watch their money in action from Friday night through Sunday. If you hold this film until a week or two before the Super Bowl you might have a blockbuster. But you are not going to get sports gamblers off the couch and into a movie theater on the first weekend in October. I may not know much about the movie business but I do know a lot about the gambling business."

There were several issues involved in the scheduling. I don't know whether it was true, but I heard there was speculation that Pacino's agent thought the role of Walter might earn Al an Academy Award nomination if the picture was in the movie houses before the end of the year. But what I believed from the start was that Jim Robinson at Morgan Creek never embraced the idea that *Two for the Money* was a gambling movie that would have a special appeal to people who bet on sporting events.

All told, the film brought in a total of only $24.9 million at the box office. I had been guaranteed $150,000 for my life rights and there were bonus clauses in my contract as well. The first bonuses for back-end money kicked in at $30 million. I was supposed to get an additional $100,000 if the movie did $35 million; $250,000 if the movie earned $40 million or more, and $500,000 for anything above $50 million. The movie remained in theaters for only five weeks and then was released in a DVD two weeks before the Super Bowl, precisely when I had suggested it ought to open in theaters. The DVD sold $19.9 million, just $5 million less than box office, which is almost unheard of. The movie would have earned at least $40 million if it had opened when the DVD was released.

My point is made even stronger if you consider the movies that opened at the same time as mine and did really well. The biggest hit was *Flight Plan*, with Jodie Foster, followed by *Wallace and Gromit: The Curse of the Were-Rabbit*, a kids' movie; and *In Her Shoes*, starring Shirley MacLaine and Cameron Diaz. I think it might be safe to say that none of those films appealed much to the sports gambling fraternity. If further evidence is needed, the television network TNT showed *Two for the Money* back-to-back at 8 and 10 PM the night before the 2008 Super Bowl between the Giants and the Patriots, and it was one of the highest-rated movie nights in that network's history. It was a perfect fit, an ideal lead-in to the most heavily bet sporting event in the world. Anyway, my movie career, such as it was, was over and now it was time to get back to business.

15

BACK TO BASICS

Actually, I had been edging back into the handicapping business in the three years leading up to the release of *Two for the Money*. In 2003 I had received a call from Walter about going to work for him on an Internet pick site. Internet pick sites, where you go online and buy the selections of a professional handicapper, were just coming into vogue around that time, and Walter had hooked up with a guy by the name of Steve Budin. Budin had started one of the first offshore sports books in Panama in the late nineties. It was a new idea then and it caught the eye of the government, and the feds shut them down during one of their anti-gambling campaigns. But before long, the boom came. Gambling sites were opening up in Costa Rica and everywhere else and offshore betting was flourishing. Steve liked to say that he built the bridge but didn't get to collect the tolls because he showed everyone how to do it yet wasn't there to profit from it. Steve and his father Dave had been big-time bookmakers; his father was one of the biggest in the business. They had made millions with their offshore sports book before the U.S. government closed the operation. Now, Steve was starting from scratch, selling picks on the Internet, and who better to build your empire around than the guy whose life was about to hit the big screen.

At that time I knew that the movie was going to be made and I was trying to position myself to cash in on the publicity. Had Budin not been involved, I would not have gone in with Walter because I didn't trust him, and as it turned out my instincts were sound. It did not take long before he stiffed me out of the bonus money he had promised me when we got started. I responded in kind. I cut Walter out and tied in with Budin. We hired publicists and I launched the BrandonLang.com Web site at around the time the movie was released. I had been making picks on a limited basis over the past five years and so I was up-to-date in every sport and ready to get going full time in 2005. It was a whirlwind endeavor. I seemed to be everywhere at once: I was doing radio and TV; flying to New York to do Steven A. Smith's *Quite Frankly* show on ESPN2; I'm on their *Cold Pizza* show whenever a gambling story breaks; back making big money, wearing tailored suits. I was Mike Anthony again, but in a different light. I was the new Nick the Greek.

My schedule was frenetic, and still is. With a stand-alone Web site, you have to be doing something every day. I have to pick the games, post them on the Web site, and of course it has to be updated every day. But it's far better than working the phones. I never have to speak to anyone personally. There are no Amirs that I have to concern myself with. Clients sign up on a daily, weekly, monthly, or annual basis. It's a simple procedure. You go online and go to my Web site. If you want the day's plays, you punch in your credit card number and buy the day's package for $34.95. Then you bet the games any way you choose. You can bet them legally in Vegas or you can go offshore or bet with your local bookmaker. I have nothing to do with any of that. I just give you my picks and what you do with them is up to you. It's not like when I was working for Walter. I'm not a salesman now. I don't have to try to push you to bet more than you're comfortable betting. You play it however you want to and my conscience is clear.

I recently moved from Vegas to Florida because so much of my radio and TV business is in the East. I fly to Philadelphia on Wednesday nights and do my best to relax. I wake up Thursday morning to a hectic routine. I do twenty radio shows throughout the day in different markets around the country. I start off doing a Fox national show with Steve Zaban at 7:45 AM, then run through nineteen more, ending with Portland at 5:30 PM. On Thursday nights late in the season I'll have a nice dinner, then go to my hotel room and watch the Thursday night NFL game on the NFL Network. I don't watch a game like the average fan does. I scout it. I watch it and analyze it from many different perspectives. How is the offensive line playing? Is the defense putting pressure on the quarterback? How are the corners and safeties covering? How does the quarterback match up against this secondary? How does the offensive line match up against the defensive front? Who is controlling the line of scrimmage? How does the visiting quarterback look playing on the road in cold weather? Can the defensive backs cover the receivers man-to-man or will they need help?

One Thursday night in the 2008 season, I was watching the Cleveland Browns play the Baltimore Ravens. At the time, Cleveland was 3–4 and the Ravens were 4–3, but the Browns were a slight favorite at home. After losing their first three games, they had come back and won three of their last four, including a lopsided twenty-one-point victory over an undefeated Giants team on Monday Night Football and an impressive win over Jacksonville on the road. But as I'm watching the game I see that the Cleveland cornerback, Brandon McDonald, is being eaten alive by Baltimore receiver Derek Mason. He's playing him one-on-one and he can't cover him. I check to see who the Browns are playing the following week and learn that they will be home again against Denver. The Broncos are playing .500 ball, and being on the road they will probably be a three-point underdog to Cleveland. But the Browns are on their way to giving up thirty-seven points to a Baltimore team that normally doesn't score very much and they will definitely have pass-coverage problems.

Sure enough, Cleveland was installed as a three-point favorite. Their drubbing of the Giants, who looked like the class of the NFL going into the game, had resulted in the Browns being valued much higher than they merited. What people didn't realize was that Cleveland was coming off its bye week, they were sky-high being featured on Monday Night Football against the defending Super Bowl champions, and as an eight-point underdog, they could play with abandon, having nothing to lose. Those factors were enough to make them a three-point choice against a Denver team coming off consecutive losses to Jacksonville, New England, and Miami, two of them at home.

It's hard to say that the line-makers were off because they're not trying to pick the winner; they're looking to set a line that will draw equal action on both sides of the proposition. Minus three points made Cleveland an inviting bet and it was also good enough to attract Denver money, with the Broncos getting points from a team with a 3–5 record. But it's always the matchups that I'm looking at. I knew that Denver did not have much of a defense and would probably give up a lot of points, but I also knew that Brandon McDonald would not be able to guard Brandon Marshall, and that Mike Shanahan, the Denver head coach, would go right after him. It took a while, but that's how it played out. Cleveland led by fourteen points in the fourth quarter, but then Broncos quarterback Jay Cutler threw three touchdown passes, two against a beleaguered McDonald, including a ninety-three-yard strike to Eddie Royal and the game-winning toss to Marshall with 1:14 remaining. The Broncos won, 34–30.

That was an instance in which watching the Thursday night game closely in my hotel room paid dividends. When the game is over I go straight to bed because Friday is a day that begins early and has me going nonstop. I start the day at 8:30 AM with "The Junkies" in Washington, D.C.; at 9 I'm on radio station WIP in Philadelphia; then it's 9:20 in San Diego; 9:40, Minnesota; then Houston; Tulsa; Kansas City; and it goes on that way right through the morning. I do five more radio shows on Friday afternoon and then I go down to the Wachovia Center and tape the TV segments for my four Comcast markets—Atlanta, Washington, Sacramento, and Philadelphia. Philadelphia is the base for all my radio and TV operations because, believe it or not, Philly is the number one gambling market in America. I don't know why it's ahead of New York and way ahead of Chicago, but it is. It's a great city; I love it and I'm very well known there because of my shows. It's a rare night that I go to dinner in a popular restaurant and not have someone come up to me and introduce themselves. But on Friday night I'm done. On Saturday morning I fly home to Florida and begin to sweat out the weekend's games.

Right now, I have anywhere from 5,000 to 10,000 clients, most of them weekly or monthly subscribers, depending on the season. A lot of bettors stay on for a particular sport; some play throughout the football season and quit after the Super Bowl; for others it's strictly baseball or basketball. I recently added a number of other handicappers to my Web site. These were guys that I met in my travels who wanted to get into the business. Before I allowed them to tie in with me I monitored their picks for a couple of months. I told them to e-mail their picks to me along with two paragraphs explaining why they like the games. The "whys" tell me if they really know what they're doing. For example: Why are you taking New England minus three at home over Buffalo? Just saying you like New England is not enough for me. Do you like them because they're 9–0 straight up in their last nine against Buffalo and because Buffalo is coming off a tough home loss to the Jets? If you've beaten a team nine times in a row, that is definitely the right side of the game. You force Buffalo to beat a team they haven't been able to beat, and the fact that the public has moved the line from four and a half to three points tells you that you have Buffalo money out there and you want to be on the opposite side of the public line move.

If the handicapper knows what he's doing, I let him sign on. They have their own clients and I get a little piece of their action. You can keep a client for a long time if you win for him with some consistency. You try to string some winning days together and they lead to winning weeks and then to winning months. But no matter how many winning plays you give him, you can't control whether a bettor makes a profit or finishes in the red. The key to all gambling is money management. You can give a player two winners out of three picks, but his margin will depend on how he plays them. Some bettors like to play a lot of games. They might bet ten games, win seven of them and still lose money because they bet different amounts on each game. I've always advocated quality over quantity. You have to find a game you really like and make your bets around that game. Let's say you put $100 on a game you feel strongly about. If there are a few other games you like, you can bet them lighter, or put them in a parlay, and if your chief play comes in you can lose three out of four and still make money. That's how I structure everything. Find your strongest play and stay with it.

Sometimes, one game jumps off the board and recommends itself. Other times, you might be looking ahead at a particular matchup, like the Cleveland–Denver game in which the Browns couldn't cover the Broncos' receivers. Now and then, you find a team that's undefeated halfway through the season but hasn't beaten any top teams. Teams that have won seven or eight in a row are rarely made underdogs, but you know the team is overvalued and that they are not going to go undefeated. That includes the 2007 Patriots. So you wait for a game in which they are favored on the road against a fairly solid team and bet against them. That is almost always a sound play. But no matter how good a game looks, you still have to do your homework. You have to look at a game from every angle and consider every nuance. This is especially true in a game like the Super Bowl. You have two weeks to handicap it and just about every one of your clients is going to bet it. Games like that define you as a handicapper. My Super Bowl record is 17–0–2. I have not lost that game in the last nineteen seasons and my analyses have left no detail out of the handicapping process. Here is what I offered my Internet clients before the 2009 Super Bowl between Pittsburgh and Arizona, beginning with some basic hype about my Super Bowl run:

When you have the winner early, you might as well release it. I am releasing it now. Last year I released the Giants early as an eleven-point underdog, and said it would not surprise me to see them shock the world—Giants, 17–14. Two years ago I called the Colts minus-seven over the Bears with a free pick on the Under—a perfect 2–0 sweep, courtesy of 29–17, Indy. Three years ago I gave an early release of the Steelers on the money line (to win straight-up), minus four and a half, and a play on the Under; a 3–0 sweep. My Super Bowl run started in 1987 with the Giants crushing Denver. I had no play in 1995 or1996 when I was caddying and on vacation from the business of handicapping. In 1997 and 2000 there were a pair of pushes, with New England plus fourteen over

Green Bay and the Rams minus seven over Tennessee. During my undefeated run, I've had three calls that fell almost exactly on the final score—in 1991 I called the Giants outright over the Bills with a 20–17 win; when Norwood missed his kick on the last play of the game, the score was 20–19, Giants. In 1998 I missed by one point, calling Denver 34–20 over Atlanta; 34–19 was the final. Finally, in 2002, I had New England as a double-digit dog, 21–17 over St. Louis; the final was 20–17.

I made the Pittsburgh–Arizona game a fifty-dime release, which is my highest-rated play. During the season I rated six games a forty-dime release or better and delivered on all six. Why did I rate this game that high? Why not? How else would I possibly rate a game that I have never lost? Right now, 16–0–2; #17 in a row awaits you.

I followed the hype with a note to clients who had already paid me:

I've been asked many questions about never having lost this game. How have I done it? Do I have a system? What has been the biggest key to hitting the Super Bowl every year of my career? Simply put, the main key is to look at the matchup. Forget the season and look at how the teams match up in this game. You can use what happened during the regular season and the playoffs to help gauge where a team is and what its weaknesses are, but for the most part, the Super Bowl is a game all to itself, especially with two weeks to prepare. That is by far the chief factor in handicapping the game.

A second factor is: Do I feel the underdog has a shot to win the game outright? That is of critical importance because of the forty-two Super Bowls played thus far, discounting the three games that fell right on the number, the straight up winner has covered thirty-four of thirty-nine. So if I do not feel that the underdog has a chance to win the game, I stay away.

I've looked at this game from every angle possible and I keep coming back to the same conclusion—whichever quarterback plays better and does not turn the ball over, his team will win. For my money, that quarterback is Kurt Warner and not Ben Roethlisberger, who I feel is due to implode. I have seen enough from Warner in these playoffs and in the past year and a half in this Cardinals offense to jump on his bandwagon. He has faced the Steelers' defense. He faced a good Ravens defense in a road game last year. He is as comfortable as I have ever seen him. He is better now than he ever was. Experience will do that for you. So enjoy the game, folks, and what I am comfortable will be winner #17 in a row.

There was a bit of irony in my selecting the Cardinals because of my confidence in Kurt Warner. Seven years earlier, in the 2002 Super Bowl, I picked New England over the Rams because I didn't think Warner was up to the task. I was still caddying at the time, and Mike Cruz came up to me one day and told me that a group of high-end players, led by a fellow called Big Sid, were coming in from Chicago and were scheduled to play on the morning of Super Bowl Sunday and he wanted me to wait for the call.

While playing golf at $10,000 a hole, Sid and his pals were of a mind to talk a little football. The Rams were a solid fourteen-point favorite over New England, and they were ready to lay the points. I was certain it would be a mistake. I thought the Rams were vastly overrated and that the Patriots were a good bet to win the game straight-up. The Rams had a high-octane offense—it was called the Greatest Show on Turf—and they rolled up the points all season long, but they had struggled against teams with good defenses, and New England had as good a defense as there was in the league at the time. I pointed that out to Big Sid and his pals and then went into some detail. I told them that you could count on New England's head coach, Bill Belichick, to come up with a defense that would totally confuse Kurt Warner. There was a reason that, before being picked up by the Rams, Warner had been playing in the arena league, NFL Europe, and bagging groceries in Iowa. There was a reason he hadn't been able to make it in the NFL. He had put up big numbers with the Rams because he had gotten into a system that was perfect for him—indoors, on the carpet, with a quick passing game. He could throw to a spot, to a window, and let the receiver take off from there. When the Rams won the Super Bowl two years earlier, against Tennessee, everything had fallen in their favor. Now, they were facing one of the best defensive coaches in history, and you're asking him to cover a two-touchdown spread. It's just not going to happen. I offered them this advice over the first four holes, and they were looking at me like I was a rocket scientist. Then they realized who I was. They knew me as Mike Anthony and they had gotten my play of the year, with a full explanation, free of charge. They took good care of me at the end of the round and they had no reason to regret their investment. The Patriots won the game outright, 20–17.

But seven years is a long time in the life of an athlete. Warner had matured and his head now was as good as his arm. He got rid of the ball a lot quicker. He seemed immune to the pressure of the pass rush. And most important of all, he no longer threw the ball to receivers who were well covered or put it on the ground so often. So Warner now was the main reason for my picking the Cardinals to win the game. My final release to my subscribers was an in-depth analysis of the game. It went like this:

> *Don't be surprised to see the Cardinals shock the world and win this game outright. I said the same thing last year with the eleven-point underdog Giants. They didn't disappoint me and I am confident that Arizona won't either. People often ask me about the Giants call. They ask if I could name one thing that got me on*

the Giants and my answer is always the same: I just couldn't see the Patriots blowing out the Giants, and quite frankly, I don't see the Steelers blowing out the Cardinals in this game. In picking the Giants, I said that if they don't lose the turnover battle they would give themselves a shot to win the game. As it turned out, both teams turned the ball over just once.

In their last eleven games, the Cardinals are 11–0 straight-up and 10–1 against the spread when they have a turnover advantage. When they lose the turnover battle, they are 1–7 and 1–6–1. When the teams last met, in Arizona in week four a year ago, the Cards upset the Steelers, 21–14, with each team turning the ball over twice. With a few exceptions, the rosters of both teams are pretty much the same.

There also are a number of intangibles worth considering. It starts with the Cardinals' head coach, Ken Whisenhunt, who had been offensive coordinator of the Steelers and who has an exhaustive knowledge of everything Pittsburgh does defensively, thanks to his close friendship with Dick LeBeau, the Steelers' defensive coordinator. Some might say that LeBeau is equally familiar with what Whisenhunt does on offense, but Whisenhunt did not have the weapons in Pittsburgh that he has now. He also didn't have Todd Haley, as hot an offensive coordinator as the playoffs have ever seen. The Cardinals are the first team in NFL history to put up thirty points in three consecutive playoff games. Also, Whisenhunt knows Ben Roethlisberger better than any coach in the league, better even than Roethlisberger's head coach, Mike Tomlin. After the Steelers drafted Ben, it was Whisenhunt who taught him everything about the offense; he molded him into a winning quarterback and therefore knows his every weakness.

Another coaching advantage for Arizona is that their assistant coach, Russ Grimm, used to be the offensive line coach in Pittsburgh and is familiar with LeBeau's defensive line and blitzing schemes. And the Cards' offensive line started all nineteen games this season, unprecedented in the NFL. Finally, six other Cardinals coaches have ties to the Steelers; people have actually been calling Arizona the "Steelers of the West." Information like that is priceless when you have two weeks to prepare.

It's true that the Steelers have the best overall defense in the league, but they haven't faced an offense like this one all year, especially an offense that is peaking at exactly the right time with a quarterback playing the best ball of his entire career. Think about this: the Eagles came into Arizona to play for the conference championship with the third best defense in the NFL and the Cards shredded them throughout the entire first half. Did they ease up in the second half? You bet they did and who could blame them, being up 24–6. But when the game was on the line, Warner led them on the winning drive as cool and as calm as could be.

As for the Steelers' offense, it has been inconsistent all year and it's an offense against which the Cardinals *match up very well. Theirs is a much underrated defensive line that can rush the quarterback, and the Steelers' offensive line has allowed Roethlisberger to be sacked more than any other quarterback in the NFL. The Cardinals will get at least three sacks on Sunday.*

Where I think people who like Pittsburgh are missing this game is thinking that the Steelers' defense is just going to shut down Arizona on a neutral field. They also think the Steelers' offense is going to roll over the Cardinals. How overrated is the Pittsburgh offense? It scored ten points at Cleveland, six at Philly, fourteen at home against the Giants, eleven at home to the Chargers, fourteen at Tennessee, and thirteen at home to Dallas. The Steelers' offense has had the benefit of a defense that has consistently given it great field position with stops and turnovers. You also can't discount what Arizona did defensively in the second half of the Atlanta game, the entire Carolina game, and the first half of the Eagles game. It is a defensive line that has been together the last four years.

In conclusion, the Cardinals will not be intimidated by anything Pittsburgh does on Sunday. This is a confident football team, led by confident coaches who believe their team will win. Of all the teams the Steelers could have played in the Super Bowl, Arizona is the team that matches up best against them across the board. In a game like this, with teams more evenly matched than people think, your value is with the underdog, getting six and a half points, and a quarterback who, with a

win on Sunday, punches his ticket to the Hall of Fame.
This game will go down to the wire. Perhaps the last
team with the ball gets it done; but there will be no
blowout in what I feel will be a field goal game. My
seventeenth straight Super Bowl winner is Arizona
plus the points.

As a bonus, I advised bettors to play Arizona on the
money line, getting close to two-to-one odds that the
Cardinals win the game outright. The final score, I said,
would be 23–20, and with less than a minute to play, I
had it right on the nose. A Pittsburgh touchdown with
thirty-five seconds to go cost me the money-line bet and
the satisfaction of nailing the exact score.

The narrow miss took me back to the 1999 Super
Bowl between Denver and Atlanta. At the time I was
still caddying and trying to get a movie made. I watched
the game at a big celebrity party in the five-level Bel Air
mansion of Freddy DeMann, the film producer and music
executive. Bruce Jenner and Sugar Ray Leonard were
there, along with other movers and shakers from the worlds
of show biz and sports. I got there at about eleven in the
morning, with my buddy Chris Case, and by kickoff time
we were three sheets to the wind. Feeling nice and loose,
I stood up before the entire party in Freddy's film room
and announced that the final score of the game would
be Denver 34, Atlanta 20. Then I told Freddy to call his
bookmaker and bet $500 that the coin toss would come
up heads. When the coin went up in the air, the room was

as quiet as a church and when it came down heads there was a big roar and that set the tone of the party.

I had Denver to cover the spread and that bet appeared to be safe with the Broncos ahead 31–6 with five minutes to go, but my final score prediction was looking way off. Not so fast. The Falcons scored to make it 31–13. Denver recovered the onside kick and a chip-shot field goal pushed the score to 34–13. On an incredible drive, Atlanta picked up three fourth-down conversions and scored with thirty-eight seconds left to make the score 34–19. The extra point would put me right on the money, and everyone was asking me, "How did you know?" But Dan Reeves, the Atlanta coach, decided to go for a two-point conversion, so whether they converted it or not, I'd miss by a point. Why go for the two? One way or the other, he will still need two touchdowns; is losing 34–21 more satisfying than losing 34–20? Anyway, they didn't convert and 34–19 was the final.

Now fast-forward to the 2009 Super Bowl. I thought we might replay a bit of the past and I called Chris and said let's get the old gang together again at his place. This time it wasn't a celebrity gathering like the one in 1998, just some friends and Freddy's family, but once again I offered a forecast of the final score: Arizona 23, Pittsburgh 20.

As the game unfolds, it's 10–7 Steelers late in the second quarter and the Cardinals are driving, but Warner is intercepted by linebacker James Harrison, who returns the interception the length of the football field for a remarkable touchdown as time expires. Quick as that, I'm down 17–7.

Back to Basics

It looks bad and I'm feeling suicidal. I step outside and walk around aimlessly, trying to clear my head, and when I come back into the house things are looking even worse. Arizona has gone three-and-out and Pittsburgh has the ball first-and-goal at the Cardinals eight. I'm saying to myself that if the score goes to 24–7, the Cards will not recover and my Super Bowl run will be over. At this point, I'm no longer watching the game with the crowd on the big screen. I'm in the kitchen, watching it on a fourteen-inch screen with two Hispanic bus boys and the maid, but it's working out all right because the Steelers drive stalls and they're going for a field goal. I'm superstitious, so I stay in the kitchen, but on fourth down the Cardinals rough the placeholder and Pittsburgh is rewarded with a new set of downs at the Cardinals three. On first down, a Roethlisberger pass is tipped and almost intercepted, and I said right then that they won't pass again. I remembered that when the Steelers won the Super Bowl in '05, Roethlisberger threw a pick in the third quarter that led to a touchdown and almost cost them the game. So they run the ball twice, the second time on a quarterback draw, and end up settling for the field goal; it's 20–7, still a two-score game. I high-five the bus boys and kiss the maid on the cheek. The karma seems to be in my favor, but Arizona is forced to punt and Pittsburgh gets to midfield before two consecutive sacks set them back and the drive fizzles. The Cardinals take possession on their own fifteen and march down the field. A one-yard Warner to Larry Fitzgerald touchdown pass makes it 20–14.

Up until that point, I had been thinking only about covering the spread and keeping my streak alive. But with the game one point under the number with five minutes left, it dawns on me that I have a chance to win the game outright. Two possessions later, Arizona is stopped, punts, and the ball is batted out of bounds at the Steelers' one-yard-line. Now, I'm looking at a live possibility of winning the game straight up and hitting my predicted 23–20 final score. I'm thinking safety and touchdown. The safety comes quickly. Center Justin Hartwig is flagged for holding in the end zone, and the resulting safety makes the score 20–16. I'm a touchdown away from a trifecta: cover the spread, win straight-up on the money line, and hit the score on the nose. Pittsburgh kicks off after the safety and on the first play from scrimmage, Fitzgerald catches a Warner pass over the middle and scoots sixty-four yards to the end zone. After the extra-point the score is 23–20 and I think we're home free, but then it hits me; there's too much time left. There's still 2:39 to go. Then I made a mistake that still haunts me. With the clock winding down, I left my Spanish contingent in the kitchen and went into the main room and there I watched the Steelers mount their game-winning drive. Wideout Santonio Holmes scores on a beautiful six-yard toe-tapper in the back of the end zone with thirty-five seconds on the clock to win it for Pittsburgh. The final score: Pittsburgh 27, Arizona 23.

I know it's insane, but to this day, I believe that had I remained with the kitchen help there is no way Pittsburgh goes on that final drive. The gambling gods taught me a lesson. The game had turned in my favor when I was watching it on the small screen with the kitchen help, but when I needed them most I went back out with the rich people and that last score was my penalty. For future reference, when I'm watching a game with the help, I stay with the help; even if I have to do the dishes, I remain in the kitchen.

When the game was over, Freddy DeMann walks up to me, puts his arm around me, and says, as only he can, "B-man, you were two minutes and thirty-nine seconds away from immortality." And isn't that the truth. But there was, after all, some consolation. When all was said and done, my Super Bowl record went to 17–0–2. The streak lives.

CHANGING SEASONS

Waking up on the morning after the Super Bowl is like awakening from a dream. The exhilaration that comes with having extended my undefeated streak to nineteen years is dampened by a feeling of exhaustion, an emotional letdown that begs for respite, and wanting nothing more than to be left alone for a few days. But it's Monday morning now and I realize that although the seasons have changed, my clients make the switch seamlessly. It's the first week of February, so we're just weeks away from the college basketball conference tournaments which leads us into March Madness. That means I have to dive right into college hoops. Fortunately, I've taken the time in December and January to handicap the teams so that I'm not starting from scratch. As a handicapper, you really don't have a committed basketball clientele when the football season is in progress. Football trumps all the other sports when it comes to gambling, but you can't wait until the season's over to begin handicapping basketball. There are too many teams and too many conferences and you have to set aside time to monitor the field while the football season is in full swing. I try not to miss a beat, to build some momentum heading into the NCAA tournament which, from a handicapper's point of view, is the greatest three-week sporting event in the country. You have the matchups of teams that might never have met before, the point spreads rising and falling, the soaring emotions, the win-or-go-home format, every game on TV, action all day long; and you have your brackets. People who don't know a pick-and-roll from an egg roll are filling out brackets and rooting for their teams; and of course there is the daily betting on the individual games.

My radio and TV schedules are off the charts during this time, especially on the weekends of the first two rounds. I move from one to the other trying to bring order to a panorama that thrives on chaos. You have to figure that somewhere along the way a team from a mid-major conference—the Horizon League, the MAC, maybe Mountain USA, a team from the Missouri Valley or the Colonial Conference—is going to upset a team from a big-power conference. In 2007 Virginia Commonwealth beat perennial powerhouse Duke on a late jumper. That same year, tiny Davidson College made it all the way to the Midwest regional final before losing to Kansas, the eventual national champion. Led by their star scorer, Stephen Curry, they knocked off Gonzaga, Georgetown, and Wisconsin in the process. And in 2006 George Mason, a team from the unheralded Colonial Conference, took down mighty UConn in overtime and made it all the way to the Final Four. They had never before advanced beyond the first round in three previous trips to the tournament.

I begin handicapping the tournament games as soon as the seedings are announced. I make my own line for every game and match it against the official line that comes out of Vegas. I look for games in which there is a large disparity between the two lines. Let's say, for example, that I have Cleveland State getting four and a half points from Wake Forest, and the line comes out at eight and a half. Cleveland State becomes a solid play. If I have LSU minus five and a half against Butler and LSU comes up favored by two and half, then LSU is a play. The line disparity is the first thing that tells me I'm on the right side of the game. If the line is not in my favor, I generally stay away from the game.

From there, I turn to the conferences. I place little significance in what happens in the conference tournaments because the teams within the conferences play one another regularly and they're familiar with their opponents' systems. What you really have to handicap thoroughly in the first two rounds of the tournament are the bracket-buster games. You have to take a close look at games between teams from different conferences, particularly those that are played late in the season. You also have to realize that almost all tournament games are being played on a neutral floor; there are few games where a team has home-court advantage. But you have to be aware of it when it does happen. Some teams play well on a neutral floor, while others prefer home cooking. If a team plays well away from home and if it hangs tough with teams in higher rated conferences, it figures to be a good play in the tournament. For example, East Tennessee State was competitive all season long against teams from outside its conference, but in the 2009 tournament it was catching twenty-one points from Pittsburgh, the number one seed in the East region. ETSU had three incredible scorers and they played Pitt tough the whole way, easily covering the spread.

You also have to examine a team's roster, especially its starting lineup. You match their box score from an early season game against its most recent game. Circumstances change in the course of a season and you want to be sure you are handicapping the same team in March that looked impressive in January. There may be a different point guard running the team now and that can make a vast difference. You also want to know if the change was made by choice or necessity; was it intended to improve the team's performance or was the starting guard injured? You have to know your personnel. How many starters returned from last year's team and how far did that team go? You have to match last year's numbers with the numbers they're putting up this year. Has a new scorer emerged? Has the sixth man off the bench become a starter? You have to dig deep when handicapping the NCAA tournament because you know the line-makers in Las Vegas don't do that. They're setting the line where they think they can attract equal action on both sides of the game. This sometimes leads to bad lines, and bad lines are what we're looking for.

In the 2009 tournament, American University returned four of its five starters from the previous year. They were a solid basketball team and they were getting seventeen and a half points from Villanova. The line was set extra high because the game was being played at the Wachovia Center in Philadelphia, which is basically a home floor for Villanova. American had played well away from home all season and the line was much too high. The underdog had a twelve-point lead in the second half, but Villanova turned it on in late in the game and won by thirteen. At no point did I think American would fail to cover.

The line disparity between Cleveland State and Wake Forest made Cleveland State an easy choice despite the thirteen versus four seed matchup, and a look at their personnel reinforced the pick. Cleveland State was a disciplined team composed mostly of seniors who had been there before, and they played great man-to-man defense. Wake Forest was a good team from a power conference, but they were young and when the line dropped a full point to seven and a half, it told me that Cleveland State was a good bet. Did I see the upset coming? No, but I let the line do the talking.

Sorting out the teams, looking for the jewel lost in the debris, is a time-consuming and demanding process. The hot mid-major conferences change from year to year. In '08 there were four Missouri Valley teams in the field; in '09 there was none. This year there was no George Mason or Davidson lurking in the wings. Western Kentucky might have filled that role. They had a late lead against Gonzaga, but lost on a layup at the buzzer. There are not enough hours in the day to handicap sixty-three games over a three-week period, and the early rounds are especially difficult because there are a lot of games and a lot of teams that you have not seen and know little about. That's why it's important to study as much as you can during the season. The small-conference tournaments can usually be found on cable TV, and you have to try to watch them, evaluate the teams' personnel, and ask yourself how they might match up with a Duke, Villanova, UConn, or that number one seed they're going to see in the second round if they happen to get by their first-round opponent.

There are no such mysteries, no hidden entities, when it comes to handicapping the NBA. All the teams are right there in the open, they've been playing one another all year, you're familiar with every player on every team's roster, and that might lead you to believe that it's easier to pick winners in the NBA. It's not. The problem with gauging the relative merits of two teams about to play each other is that you have no way of knowing whether the teams come into the game ready to play. It's a long, grinding season in which teams play three or four games a week—sometimes playing each game in a different city—and it's impossible to be prepared to compete in every game. In my opinion, the NBA is all about emotional intensity. I've partied with enough of those guys in Las Vegas over the years to know that there are instances during the season where they just don't care about the game. That's why you can see a thirty-one-point lead with five minutes to go in the third quarter disappear in the fourth. You can't handicap emotional intensity and that's what makes it so difficult to handicap the NBA night after night. How come the Los Angeles Lakers can go into Minnesota well-rested and be down five points in the fourth quarter when two weeks earlier they went into the same city on back-to-back nights and blew the Timberwolves out by twenty points? You've got to tread lightly during the regular NBA season and pick your spots. You have to know when a team is playing for something and how rested they are before you get to analyzing how the teams match up with each other.

All of that changes when you get to the playoffs, though. There, every game means something; that's where you find the emotional intensity. It's easy to figure out how the teams match up because they played each other during the regular season and they might even have met in the previous year's playoffs. There are no surprises. You are familiar with the players on both teams, you know if there's any bad feeling between them, you know their systems and what they like to do. So you begin by looking for line value. You watch for line moves; are they smart-money moves or public moves?

It's much easier to determine the right side of a game in the playoffs, especially in the early rounds. As the series progresses there are additional circumstances that must be considered. If a team is down three games to one and is coming home they tend to be a good bet. If the line is favorable, particularly if the home team is getting points, hammer it. They don't want to lose the series in their own building, so their intensity should be at a peak. If they had played well in their three losses, they might believe they still have a chance to win the series. If, on the other hand, they were blown out in two of those games, you have to be careful, because if they feel they have no chance of beating the other team three times in a row, they might be eager to save themselves a trip back to the other city and come out flat.

I usually do pretty well in the NBA playoffs by watching the game-by-game progression. You see certain things taking place. If you understand basketball, you watch game one and see what adjustments the losing team might be looking to make in game two. An example of the kind of missteps you look for is the opening game of the Suns–Spurs series in the 2008 NBA playoffs. As I recall it, the Suns were up three with fifteen seconds to go. They're about to steal game one at San Antonio and if they do they'll be in great shape to win the series. There's a timeout, the Spurs have the ball, and they need a three-point shot to tie the score to force overtime. Mike D'Antoni, then the Phoenix Suns' coach, looks at star power forward Amare Stoudemire and says, "Listen, if they run Michael Finley off your guy, if they pick the guy you're defending, when Finley goes by you have to step out and defend the three-point line; a two-point basket does them no good." Stoudemire nods his head. Now the play starts and sure enough, Finley comes off the pick but instead of stepping out to the three-point line to guard Finley, Stoudemire stays with the man who set the pick. If he had followed Finley to the three-point line and put a hand in his face, Tony Parker, who had the ball, would have had to launch a three with Steve Nash right in his grill. But because Stoudemire doesn't stay with Finley he has a wide open shot and he hits it to tie the score and send the game into overtime.

Now, Phoenix has a three-point lead with the ball and thirty-six seconds to go in the first overtime period. They run the shot clock down to four and Stoudemire flashes into the lane and he's got a short jumper with about fifteen seconds left. If he makes the shot, the Suns will have a five-point lead and likely take game one. But instead of shooting, Stoudemire puts the ball on the floor, attacks the rim, and gets called for charging. It's his sixth foul and he's out of the game. The Spurs take possession, Tim Duncan hits a rare three and the Suns eventually lose in double overtime.

After watching the first game it was pretty clear to me that the Suns had shot their load and were pretty much done in the series. They were drained emotionally and they never recovered. They lost the series four games to one. That's how important emotional intensity is in an NBA series.

Of all the sports, I've had more success with baseball than any of the others. It's the easiest to handicap. You don't have to concern yourself with giving or getting points and there are no line moves to follow. Just pick the winner of the game. With baseball, you're dealing almost exclusively with money odds. If a team is a 150 favorite, it means you have to bet $150 to win $100. Of course if you bet the underdog you will get back only $130 for a $100 bet, the difference being the vigorish, which is taken in dollars rather than in points. There are run lines as well—teams favored by a run and a half or two runs—but it's the money line that sets the price of the game. In sports like football and basketball, which are governed by the point spread, you're always laying 10 percent vigorish; you put up $110 to win $100. But with baseball the amount you need to wager to win $100 is determined by the money line as it is set in Vegas.

The cardinal rule when betting baseball is that you never bet a favorite of more than 150 unless you balance it with a bet on the run line. For example, if you like a team that is a 160 favorite, you never bet it straight. You lay the run and a half which brings your bet down to about even money, or pick 'em. The difference is that if your team wins by one run you lose your bet. It's something to consider but not for very long because if you don't think your team is good enough to win by two runs or more you shouldn't be betting it.

The best bets in baseball are almost always underdogs. It's a game of streaks. Even bad teams usually go on a winning streak some time during the season and good teams go on losing streaks, so you watch for the streaks and you ride them. But you have to pay close attention to the odds. When a good team has ripped off four or five in row, the money line will keep rising and you will have to spot a few runs to keep the price in check. If you can get a 220 favorite down to minus 130 by laying a couple of runs, it's a much better value. Statistically, very few games are decided by one run. Here's a stat that might surprise you: In about half the games played over the course of a season, the winning team will score as many runs in a single inning as the losing team will in the whole game. Of course that stat can as easily work against you as for you. There *are* games that are decided by one run and they can torment you when you play the run line.

For example, in July of 2008 Rich Harden was traded from the A's to the Cubs. He was having a pretty good year, and in his first start at Wrigley Field he faced the punchless San Francisco Giants. The Cubs were minus 230; I loved Harden going at home, and I laid a run and a half which brought my bet down to minus 125. I thus increased the value of the favorite by more than $100, but now I needed the Cubs to win by at least two runs. They were up 7–1 at the end of seven innings and my bet was looking good. But once Harden passed the one hundred-pitch mark, the game was turned over to the bullpen and a procession of relief pitchers gave up six runs in the top of the eighth to tie the score. The Cubs scored a run to win it in the bottom of the eleventh but it wasn't good enough; I lost my run-line bet.

Another way of increasing the value of your bet if you like a few favorites is to play them in a parlay; that will usually reduce the odds to about even money. While it's true that if you lose one game in a parlay you lose your whole bet, you still might be better off than betting the games individually, for if the money line is high enough, it's possible to lose on one game more than twice what you win on the other.

Handicapping a baseball game begins, and often ends, with assessing the pitchers and how they match up with the opposing team. Some pitchers have great records against a particular team for reasons that cannot be easily explained. For instance, Roy Oswalt of the Astros is 23–1 in twenty-six career starts against the Cincinnati Reds. While that's an extraordinary case, you can find other plays like that if you dig and do your homework. A pitcher's record against a particular team is one factor; others are his record in each ballpark, how he pitches on three days rest, whether he seems to pitch better at night or in day games. If you spend the time to chart such items and bet wisely you can be very successful betting baseball.

The pitcher is almost always the key. But handicapping the pitcher has become more difficult in recent years because, for the most part, starters are not allowed to finish games anymore. The complete game, once a standard statistic when evaluating a pitcher, is now about as extinct as eight-track tapes. Now you have to spend as much time analyzing the bullpen as you do the starter. It's not just the closer, either. It's the long man, the setup man, the left-handed specialist who comes in to pitch to just one left-handed batter. The pitch count, a figure that didn't even exist twenty years ago, is now as critical as a pitcher's earned run average. A pitcher who passes the one hundred-pitch mark is looking over his shoulder at the action in the bullpen even if he's pitching a three-hit shutout. Still, it would not be so difficult to handicap if you were dealing with one reliever, or even two. But now you have managers mixing and matching. It hardly matters how well a pitcher is pitching. If it's late in the game and a left-handed batter is coming up against your right-handed pitcher, more likely than not, the manager will go to the bullpen for a lefty.

Early in the 2009 season, the Yankees' manager, Joe Girardi, offered an illustration of how to blow a game by overmanaging your pitching staff. Joba Chamberlain, whom Girardi and his staff coddle like an overprotected child, had pitched six innings and given up one earned run. But eighty-eight pitches in one game was deemed enough and Brian Bruney was called upon to protect a one-run lead. Bruney pitched a perfect seventh, but not perfect enough to remain in the game. With two left-handers due up, Damaso Marte was summoned; he retired both. But a right-hander was due up next, so Jose Veras was hailed and he put the tying run on base with a walk. Now came a left-hander and in came Phil Coke, who had looked like a batting practice pitcher in an earlier outing, and he reinforced the image by giving up three hits and two runs before getting the third out of the inning. The Yanks lost by two runs because percentage-playing, push-button managing put the team's least effective pitcher in the game at its most critical juncture. Girardi is hardly the exception, either. The 2008 Mets' bullpen turned Johan Santana's first season with the team into a nightmare by blowing lead after lead when he had pitched well as the starter.

This fairly recent tendency, to use a storehouse of pitchers to close out a game, has made handicapping baseball an increasingly difficult proposition. But it still is easier than the other sports. The best advice to follow when betting on baseball is to look for the underdogs. Unlike football and basketball, there are no really shocking upsets in baseball. Over the course of a season, the best team in the league is apt to lose more than once to the worst team in its division; it might even get swept in a three- or four-game series. Top football or basketball teams will almost never lose to a bad team more than once. In addition to being a good percentage play, betting an underdog in baseball offers a good return on your investment because you are being given odds, not points.

The baseball season also offers me a bit of relief in my work schedule; for more than two months, from mid-June when the NBA season ends, until football kicks off early in September, it's the only sport I have to deal with. And I'm guaranteed to have at least two days off—the day before and the day after baseball's All-Star Game. Once September comes, I have more than one sport going at all times. It's an unrelenting business, a full-time, year-round job that offers little respite. But I love it.

ADDENDUM

THE CASE FOR SPORTS BETTING

The most compelling argument for legalizing sports betting is that there is no coherent reason for opposing it. Competitive sports are cut deep in America's psyche and betting on them is embedded in its DNA. Gambling on sporting events is proceeding in almost every state in the union at a pace that continues to grow. Estimates of how much is wagered annually run as high as $380 billion. That figure comes from the National Gaming Impact Study Commission (NGISC) in a comprehensive report authorized by an act of Congress and signed by President Clinton in 1999. While the report is ten years old, little has changed in the past decade except that the approximated figures almost certainly have grown. We know, for example, that more than $2.5 billion was wagered legally in Nevada in 2007, more than $92 million on the 2008 Super Bowl, and about twice that on the NCAA tournament. Of course those numbers apply only to the more than one hundred legal sports books in Nevada. They account for a small fraction of the total betting handle across the country, sums small and large wagered with bookmakers, in lotteries, office pools, and on the Internet. In his testimony before the Senate Commerce Committee on the Amateur Sports Integrity Act in 2001, Danny Sheridan, the nationally known oddsmaker, suggested that more than 99 percent of sports gambling takes place illegally outside of Nevada. He estimated that forty million Americans wager at least $6 billion illegally every weekend during the twenty-week college and pro football seasons alone. Those figures have no doubt been swollen by the advent of Internet betting with offshore sports books, an activity that barely existed at the turn of the decade.

The NGISC report, which covers every form of gambling everywhere in the United States, is as thorough as any subsequent report is likely to be. What it lacked, however, was any hint of objectivity. It was clearly written from a certain point of view, which is that sports betting is detrimental to the public good, particularly when the wagering is on amateur sports. One Las Vegas Strip resort is quoted as saying that about one-third of the $77.4 million wagered at its sports book was bet on college football and basketball. The point spread in those sports is cited as a contributing factor to the moral decay engendered by sports gambling. The claim made is that publicizing the spread in newspapers and on television broadcasts all over the country creates the illusion that wagering on those games is legal.

The report justifies banning sports betting while giving its imprimatur to all other forms of gambling, including the pari-mutuels at racetracks, off-track betting, state-run lotteries, and casino gambling by insisting that those activities contribute to the local economy, produce jobs, and create other economic centers. Of course the reason that sports gambling fails to meet those standards is that, being illegal, it must operate in the shadows. If it were legalized it would make entrepreneurs out of bookmakers who might employ clerks, or cashiers, to take the bets. They would operate out of offices for which they would pay rent, and as for contributing to the local economy, estimates are that sports gambling would produce tax revenues in excess of $6 billion dollars a year. That would seem to be a pretty fair contribution to the economy.

The report puts forth five issues that it deems sufficient to keep sports betting from being legalized: 1) it has the potential to devastate families and destroy careers; 2) it endangers the integrity of sports; 3) it is a threat to adolescents, noting that there are bookmakers on every campus and that college students spend more money on gambling than they do on alcohol; 4) it might introduce the involvement of organized crime; 5) it might lead to other forms of gambling.

Each of those arguments is embarrassingly flimsy. While it is true that sports betting, or any other form of gambling, can become compulsive and lead to unhappy endings, it is not likely that gambling has devastated more lives than the injudicious consumption of alcohol. Placing a bet on a ball-game does not, for example, affect one's ability to operate an automobile and that's why there is no law against gambling and driving. While no statistics have yet been compiled, it is fair to guess that cigarette smoking has killed many more people than gambling. Yet alcohol and cigarettes remain legal. Prohibiting the first has already proven to be catastrophic to the public welfare, and the second will not be banned because the tobacco lobby has too much muscle.

As for sports betting being a threat to adolescents, if there already are bookmakers on every campus, how would legal bookmakers further imperil the youth? The fact that more money is spent on gambling than on alcohol would appear to be a favorable circumstance, given the respective dangers inherent in betting and drinking. As for organized crime, it is precisely because gambling is illegal that it is often connected to organized crime; bookmaking can be neatly integrated into a criminal network that already traffics in narcotics and prostitution. Transforming the bookie into the equivalent of the British turf accountant would be the surest way to keep gambling from being infiltrated by organized crime. As for betting on sports leading to other forms of gambling, like what? Lotteries, craps, blackjack? Such activities are already widely available to those who are inclined to bet a few bucks here or there. As for lotteries, which come in as many flavors as ice cream, states not only encourage them, they spend millions of taxpayer dollars promoting them on television. Incidentally, what exactly is the difference between the numbers racket and a round of lotto you can watch live on TV as the winning numbers spin into place?

The heart of the argument against sports gambling is what the report calls "the integrity of sports." It is the injunction by which the professional sports leagues and the NCAA stake their claim on the pristine quality of their operations. Of course the bane of any sport is the prospect that a game might be fixed. Baseball suffered a nearly fatal blow during the Black Sox scandal of 1919. The game had to be completely refashioned in order to restore fan interest. College basketball scandals in 1951 and 1961 left the sport limping until the expansion and marketing of the NCAA tournament restored it to life. Ironically, it was bracketology—the ubiquitous filling out of tournament brackets and wagering a sum on the outcome, illegal in most states—that rejuvenated interest in the college game and propelled it to new heights. It was illegal gambling that lifted college basketball to the level of the Super Bowl and the World Series in national attention. It is also illegal gambling that made pro football America's game. Monday Night Football and the newly minted Thursday night games that are carried on the NFL's own network would not last a season if it were not possible to get down a bet on the games.

It appears to be something of a paradox that the organizations that profit most from sports betting are those who voice the strongest opposition. But a closer look reveals that such a two-edged stance serves them well at both ends; it allows leagues to claim allegiance to the angels while the devil pays their way. They lament the odds-setting, the point spreads, the handicapping, and the large sums of money that change hands quickly on the turn of athletic fortune. At the same time they profit hugely from the enterprise they are condemning. Atop a mountain of self-righteous hypocrisy, they proclaim their innocence while building new stadiums and arenas with the funds—both public and private—pouring into their coffers. These sports organizations constitute an ad hoc lobby that puts the pressure on clueless politicians who are never reluctant to parade their purity of soul before the voting public.

The virtue of keeping sports unblemished and as immune to the fix as possible is unquestioned. What is overlooked by those who declaim against sports betting is that making it legal will offer a degree of protection that does not currently exist. The first indication that someone might be tampering with the outcome of a game is a fluctuation in the odds or the point spread. Sudden line moves, particularly late in the betting process, suggest that certain interests might be looking to guarantee the outcome of a game. Contrary to popular belief, bookmakers are the most endangered species if a contest is fixed. Small-time bookies have been put out of business when too much capital was invested on one side of the proposition before they were able to adjust their line. In 1950, a year before the first major point-shaving scandal occurred in college basketball, it became nearly impossible to get a bet down on LIU (Long Island University), which was arguably the best team in the country. Bookmakers regularly pulled their games—one was told simply that LIU was listed as "off"—and so everyday bettors understood that games were being fixed long before the authorities expressed any suspicion.

Addendum: The Case for Sports Betting

Being aware of the line moves—how quickly they rose or fell and how often—was, in an inverted sense, the equal of insider trading on Wall Street. Those on the inside— the bookie and his clients—knew more about what the future likely held than the public or even those who might be covering the games. If betting were legal, the lines would be monitored, as the stock market is supposed to be, and any suggestion of foul play would be investigated by those charged with overseeing the operation. It would offer a measure of protection to the betting public and serve as a deterrent to anyone looking to game the system.

Currently, gambling on sports is legal in only three states other than Nevada—Montana, Oregon, and Delaware. Those three were grandfathered in under a 1992 federal law that made it illegal for states that had never permitted sports betting to introduce it. The action in Montana and Oregon has so far been inconsequential. Montana allows NCAA bracket pools in bars that register with the state's lottery. Oregon ran a sports lottery for a while but dropped it when the NBA threatened to keep all postseason games away from the state.

Until just two weeks before the opening of the 2009 football season, Delaware's plans to legalize sports betting appeared to be a sure thing. But a federal appeals court tipped the odds in the other direction, and when all was said and done, Delaware lost more than it had bargained for. The prospects looked bright in May when the state passed a bill making it legal to bet on sports events. The only question at the time was whether the state constitution permitted straight betting—a bet on the outcome of a single game—or only proposition bets—chiefly parlays and lotteries, in which the bettor must pick the winners in two or more games. Governor Jack Markell favored straight betting because that's where the action was and it was estimated that it would produce some $52 million in state funds.

Within two months, the NFL, joined by Major League Baseball, the NBA, the NCAA, and the National Hockey League, filed suit in Wilmington seeking a preliminary injunction banning Delaware from taking bets on its games. The basis for the suit was that the state law allowing sports gambling violated the Professional & Amateur Sports Protection Act (PASPA) of 1992, a federal law that prohibits states from taking bets on sporting events. The trial court rejected the motion for a preliminary injunction, holding that the leagues had failed to show that any "irreparable harm" would result if single-game betting were allowed. The plaintiffs filed an appeal with the 3rd Circuit Court of Appeals.

At this point, the prospect of legalized straight betting appeared to be a pretty safe bet. Governor Markell had already received an advisory opinion from the Delaware Supreme Court to the effect that the new law would not violate the state constitution. The denial of the request for an injunction in the federal trial court seemed to further strengthen the defendant's case. But the three-judge panel for the appeals court took a harder line than anyone had expected. They ruled unanimously that there were no factual questions at issue and that, "as a matter of law," Delaware's proposal to expand sports betting beyond what was permitted under the grandfather clause would be a violation of PASPA. The appellate court not only overturned the lower court's refusal to grant a preliminary injunction, it ruled that a permanent injunction should be issued. The only recourse left to the state was to seek to have the case reargued before all twelve active judges in the 3rd Circuit, but the likelihood of a reversal appeared dim.

New Jersey also met the standard prescribed by PASPA's grandfather clause. With its Atlantic City gaming operation, it had a long history of permitting some form of gambling. But while it met the standard, it failed the test. Twice, the State Senate, with a Democratic majority, passed bills to permit sports gambling, but they never made it to the floor of the Republican-controlled Assembly. The deadline to enact such a measure, January 1, 1994, passed with no action taken. Fifteen years later, the state revived its quest.

In the spring of 2009, the initiative was resurrected, not in the state legislature but in federal court. State Senator Raymond Lesniak, a Democrat of Union County, along with the interactive Media Entertainment & Gaming Association (iMEGA), filed suit in U.S. District Court in Newark, charging that the 1992 act was unconstitutional. Named as defendants in the suit were U.S. Attorney General Eric Holder and Ralph Marra Jr., New Jersey's acting U.S. attorney. Specifically, the plaintiffs, represented by Lesniak's firm, Weiner Lesniak, claimed that the law violates five amendments to the U.S. Constitution:

- the Fourteenth Amendment's Equal Protection Clause because it denies some states rights that are afforded others;
- the Fifth Amendment, which guarantees due process to all persons;

- the Tenth Amendment by giving the federal government authority that is reserved to the states;
- the Eleventh Amendment, which grants sovereign immunity to the states; and
- the First Amendment because it has a chilling effect on efforts to enact legislation and regulate sports betting for the state.

If the suit were to be successful, the federal law would be overturned and each state would be left to decide the issue for itself.

Joseph Brennan Jr., chairman and CEO of iMEGA, estimated that sports gambling could become a $10 billion-a-year industry in New Jersey by 2011 if it were permitted in casinos, at racetracks, online, and by telephone. Such a figure would generate about $100 million a year in tax revenues for the state, Brennan said. But, he added, "This is about more than revenue. It's about economic activity."

The suit won the immediate support of State Senator Jeff Van Drew, who represents Atlantic City. Governor Jon Corzine, who initially said the idea of legalizing sports betting was "worth pursuing," later decided to take a more active role in seeking its passage. In August 2009 he filed a motion to intervene and join the plaintiffs. The Department of Justice responded by asking the court to block Corzine from joining the suit. In addition, two U.S. senators—Jon Kyl (R-AZ) and Orrin Hatch (R-UT)—wrote a letter to Attorney General Holder asking him to vigorously oppose the suit.

Predictably enough, the suit also was opposed by all professional sports leagues and scholastic associations. Joe

Addendum: The Case for Sports Betting

Browne, executive vice president of the NFL, said the league supported the ban on betting. "We do not believe it is in our best interests to have outside parties—whether casinos or local governments—using our games, players, and coaches as betting vehicles," he said.

The senators who supported the suit offered a practical view of the issue. "We cannot afford to be naïve about illegal sports betting," said Van Drew. "It's happening right now and is funding other criminal enterprises which are far more dangerous."

Lesniak mocked the presumed innocence of those who supported the ban, as if legalizing sports gambling would introduce a new phenomenon that would tear at the social fabric. He offered this insight: "As Captain Renault said to Rick (in the film *Casablanca*) 'I'm shocked—shocked—to find that gambling is going on here.' Gambling is going on here," Lesniak said emphatically, "sports gambling. Rather than supporting thousands of jobs, economic activity, and tourism, the federal ban supports offshore operators and organized crime." He added, "This federal law deprives the State of New Jersey of over $100 million of yearly revenues, as well as depriving our casinos, racetracks, and Internet operators of over $500 million in gross income."

Another suit filed in New Jersey, this one aimed specifically at a law against Internet betting, was turned aside by an appeals court in September 2009. Once again, the plaintiff was iMEGA. The statute that was challenged, the Unlawful Internet Gambling Enforcement Act (UIGEA) of 2006, does not make Internet gambling illegal; it targets financial institutions and transactions, making it illegal to transfer funds from financial institutions to companies engaged in "unlawful Internet gambling."

After a full year of thrust-and-parry between iMEGA and the federal government, the issue was decided by the U.S. 3rd Circuit Court of Appeals which upheld the legality of UIGEA. While rejecting the plaintiff's argument that the law was vague and an intrusion on individual privacy rights, the judges specifically noted that the legality of Internet betting depended on the law in the state where the bettor was located. The court emphasized that UIGEA did not establish an overall federal ban on Internet gambling.

Judge Dolores Sloviter wrote: "It bears repeating that the Act itself does not make any gambling activity illegal. Whether the transaction . . . constitutes unlawful Internet gambling turns on how the law of the state from which the bettor initiates the bet would treat that bet; i.e., if it is illegal under that state's law, it constitutes 'unlawful Internet gambling' under the Act."

As iMEGA's chairman, Brennan looked for a sliver of hope wherever one might be found. "The court made it clear," he said, "that gambling on the Internet is unlawful where state law says so. But there are only a half-dozen states that have laws against Internet gambling, leaving forty-four states where it is potentially lawful. It's not perfect, but it's a good start."

Brennan also held out the possibility of an appeal, pending a review of the case by iMEGA's legal team. But such a move seemed unlikely. Surely, Brennan was aware of the old gambling adage that everything in life is 6–5 against.

—S. C.

AFTERWORD

LOOKING AHEAD

It's been a long journey from Midland, Michigan, to where I am today. The road, not always smooth and marked by some sharp turns, has taken me from the Midwest to the Mid East, from Southern California to Las Vegas, from New York to Australia, back to Southern California and Las Vegas, and finally to the East Coast. I live in Florida now with my wife Kim and our daughter, Ireland Jade, who was born in the spring of 2009. I travel to Philadelphia regularly to do my television shows, but for the most part I have planted roots in an area where I can raise a family and continue to do what I do best, pick games and play pickup basketball every Wednesday night at the YMCA with former NBA star Christian Laettner. Not a bad gig after all.

Handicappers, by the nature of their trade, live in the future. I program what I've seen in the past to project what I think will happen some time later. I do the same when looking ahead in my own life. But some events cannot be imagined; they must be experienced, for they are powerful enough to change the way you feel about things and they compel you to rearrange your priorities. Such an event was the birth of my first child. Witnessing the miracle of childbirth was by far the greatest high I have ever felt. I am now responsible for my wife and daughter as well as myself, and I feel that I am entering a totally new stage of my life. The essentials, however, will remain the same. I will always be Brandon Lang, the kid from a small town in Michigan who dared to dream big dreams and turn some of them into reality.

I will continue to handicap games because, despite its hazards, picking winners has become a large part of who I am. Of course picking the occasional loser also is part of the formula. Unfortunately, it is the losses that attract the most attention. It always amazes me that you can win for someone week after week, even month after month, and hear little by way of appreciation. But hit a brief losing streak and that same client comes at you armed to the teeth. I love winning money for people, and no one is more upset than I am when I lose. But if you're picking games 363 days a year you're going to hit some rough spots, just as you would in any other line of work. One of my favorite sayings is, "This is not a sprint, it's a marathon." People who run with me are going to be happy sometimes, mad sometimes, and some of them will stop running and quit the race. But my career has been defined by hitting the big play more often than losing it, and if you parlay that with proper money management and discipline, over the long haul you will come out a winner.

While I plan to continue handicapping games, I am also looking ahead to new frontiers. I think there are more opportunities for me in the mainstream media. I'm already doing a good bit of radio and television work in cities throughout the country, but I think there is room for me to broaden my horizons and extend my reach. I believe I have the background, the experience, and the presence to do sports on network television and I aim to pursue that goal with the same commitment that got me to Hollywood.

So while the journey has been a long one, the road ahead is still wide open and stretches toward new horizons. I remember reading a quote by an author whose name I've forgotten. It said: "Happy is the man who has a dream and is willing to pay the price to make it come true." I believe I have done that, and I plan to continue to dream the dream and pay the price; the best is yet to come. You can bet on it.

SOURCES

Chapters Four, Five, and Seven:

Two for the Money screenplay, by Dan Gilroy; *Two for the Money* DVD, Dan Gilroy interview with Brandon Lang; Danny Sheridan testimony before the Senate Commerce Committee on the Amateur Sports Integrity Act (S. 718), April 26, 2001.

Chapter Eight:

O'Brien, Timothy L., *Bad Bet*, Times Books, 1998.

Addendum:

Danny Sheridan testimony; report of the National Gambling Impact Study Commission Act; "Seeing Good Odds, N. J. Senator Sues to Vacate Federal Sports Betting Ban," Michael Booth, *New Jersey Law Journal,* March 23, 2009; "New Jersey Files Suit on Sports-betting Ban," Jon Hurdle, *Yahoo! News*, March 23, 2009; "Suit Seeks National Legalization of Sports Betting," StarNewsOnline.com, March 24, 2009; *Poker News Daily:* "iMEGA Files Suit against UIGEA," Maria Del Mar, September 30, 2008; "U.S. Government Files Brief in iMEGA Appeals Case," Dan Cypra, October 31, 2008; "Govt. Issues Final Rule on UIGEA," Shari Geller, November 13, 2008.

ACKNOWLEDGMENTS

Brandon Lang:

I have been blessed to have so many people watch over me and come through for me every step of the way. All of my successes are their successes.

First and foremost I would like to say thank you to my lord and savior Jesus Christ. Through him all things are possible. I never would have been able to survive in my life let alone accomplish what I have without the foundation of Christianity. To my mom and my wife, the two most important women in my life, thank you for allowing me to be me.

Mom, thank you for all the sacrifices you made for me. All of my successes are a result of those sacrifices and I love you more than words will ever be able to say.

To my wife, thank you for dealing with the madness of having a husband who lives and dies with the results of sporting events every single night. You are and always will be the air that I breathe.

To my brother Bryan, you are the voice of reason when I've always needed it most and I cherish our bond as brothers. I am one of the luckiest guys in the world to have a brother like you.

To my sister, the best teenage cook in the country, I don't know what we would have done without you growing up. I just want you to know that the sacrifices you made for your brothers is duly noted here. I love you, sis.

To my Aunt Marilyn, you were the second mom I needed when dealing with my dad in high school. I would never have made it through without your prayers and perfect timed words of wisdom. I miss your waffles.

To my cousin Sheila, you were my introduction into the gambling world in the seventh grade. Who would have foreseen what that would lead to?

To Pastor Stan Anderson, my first father figure, I can never repay you for the difference you made in my life.

To Pastor Dennis Campbell, thanks for making following Christ in my teen years so much fun. I cherish those times forever.

To the late Chuck "Trz" Trzcinski, I only wish you could have been alive to see the success I've become. It would have made you proud.

Acknowledgments

To Coach Tom Hursey, the life lessons you taught me from basketball camp in the fourth grade right on through high school, when I played for you, molded my character into what it is today. I'm glad I still get a slice of Tina's strawberry pie once a year.

To Kenny Sanders, my running mate throughout adolescence and my great friend today, we made it buddy, just like we said we would.

To Senior Chief Mike Binder, your words of wisdom aboard the Battleship *New Jersey* helped me to understand what it was to be an adult child of an alcoholic and the damage my father did to my family. I am a better man today because of you.

To Roger "Rock" Ausburn, thanks for having my back during my three years aboard the *New Jersey* and always looking out for me. I couldn't have asked for a better friend, even to this day.

To Jeff Morrison, thank you for showing me how simple life could be at a time in my life when I was looking for answers. To Marty and Carolyn LaFave, you guys were always there for me and still are to this day. You were always my dose of reality when I needed it. Thank you for that.

To the late Eva Pack, who always had a room for me in Los Angeles after I got out of the navy and was trying to figure out what to do with my life, life was so simple then. I miss you.

To Lewis, Tony, and Fernando Jonas, thank you for adopting me as your brother, opening up your home to me and accepting me as family. The difference you made in my life at that critical time made a huge difference in accomplishing my dreams.

To John Wistrom at the Nevada Sports Schedule for hiring me at the Nevada Sports Schedule, and to Dennis Paulson for the recommendation of a lifetime.

To Brad Keiler for being there the night I met my wife. Your validation was a huge key and I thank you for it.

To Jeff Parrett, Robbie King, Mike Hilgar and the rest of my Orlando Bulldog teammates, my three years as a Bulldog were the best ever and the behind the back double play to Richie Cobb at the Slow-pitch Nationals in Gainesville will live in infamy. To Bryan Wirth, for getting me the interview at Riviera's tennis club, and to Terry Logan, for hiring me as a coordinator. It was the big break in Holllywood I needed.

To James "Buster" McCoy, my personal loan officer who got me through the toughest of times. Thank God the "Bank of Buster" was always open to me twenty-four hours a day, seven days a week.

To Libby Dubay, you were always there for me unconditionally and became like family to me. I am so lucky to have had a friend like you as I chased the dream. You were a believer who never doubted and I will always love you for that.

To Kris Gundmanson for finally giving me a shot to caddy at Riviera. Once I worked my way into the caddy shack, it was only a matter of time before things broke my way.

To Steve Cody who set up the meeting that would change my life. Way to come through for Super Caddy.

Acknowledgments

To Dan Gilroy and Rene Russo, you took a chance on me and I am forever grateful. I am honored to call you two friends for life.

To Jay Cohen, you kept the dream alive for seven years, and without you my life would never have made it to the big screen. You are my master of kwan.

To my boy Tommy O'Connell, you never doubted the dream when everyone else did. Your words of encouragement were always delivered when I needed them most, not to mention the legendary run at Roxy.

To my top dog Ted Tryba, the memories we have on the PGA tour are legendary and I will never be able to repay you for our historic run in 1999 at good old Riv. Thank you for letting me be part of history and I am confident our 61 together will not be broken.

To my regulars at Riviera who made my weekends a blast: Michael M. Robin, Chuck Colby, Jerry B. Festa, Ari Emanuel, Ron Papel, Steve Chase, the late Guy McElwaine, Ron Herman, Bob Glenn, and most importantly the "Z-man" Dick Zmuda.

To the golf starter at Riv while I was there, Mike Cruz, what you and I did together will go down in history and will never be duplicated. It was the run of all runs. Thanks, buddy.

To all the boys in the caddy shack at Riv, I consider you brothers in arms and will take with me memories to last a lifetime from our escapades on the course together.

To my business partner and friend Steve Budin, you are my crew and the only crew I will ever need. Your vision for BrandonLang.com was executed to perfection.

To Al Rolli who, despite having the worst people skills on the earth, is unparalleled when it comes to the Internet picks business. Thank you for putting Budin and me together.

To my publicists Jimmy Shapiro and Danny Zuckerman, you guys are the best in the business and I am glad you are on my team. Jimmy, my radio and TV schedule is the best in the business and Danny, thank you for making this book a reality.

To my business manager Dan "The Man" Rogers, thank god for your organizational skills. You've made my life a whole lot easier. You, too, are my master of kwan.

And I save the best for last, Stanley Cohen. This book would never have happened without you and I thank you for putting my life into words. The time we spent together was priceless. I looked forward to our conversations and meetings and miss them dearly now that we are done. I still can't believe that deli in New York didn't serve chips with that corned beef sandwich. It was an honor working with you.

Everyone above played their part while I chased my dreams and you all share in the ones I made come true. God bless you all.

Stanley Cohen:

I owe a huge debt of gratitude to Herman Graf and Mark Weinstein of Skyhorse Publishing. Mark edited the manuscript with precision and insight, improving it immensely. He and Herman displayed uncommon grace and understanding during the process of production which was a particularly difficult time for me. I thank them both.

Acknowledgments

My agent, Peter Sawyer, brought me together with Brandon and made his offices available for many days of interviews.

Jessica Diaz and Sharon Cangialosi transcribed the tapes promptly and accurately.

And of course there is the irrepressible Brandon Lang, who turned the entire process into an adventure.

GREAT BOOKS ON GAMBLING AND SPORTS

How to Beat the Pro Football Pointspread by Bobby Smith will set bettors on a confidence-building path lined with high-priority realities which for decades have flown under the typical football bettor's radar. Smith teaches his readers to look at the game with the bettor's eye instead of the fan's, and explains his theories on reasonable statistical expectations and how to challenge the oddsmakers. Smith has written a key resource for gamblers. $14.95 paperback

C.N. Richardson takes would-be winners through his eight-point system for betting. His key rules for doing a top-notch analysis of the odds include having knowledge of the trainers, limiting betting to no more than five races at any given track, and choosing exotic betting options, like trifectas, to maximize the investment's return. He also includes and explains personal idiosyncrasies like never betting on a race he can't see! $14.95 paperback

Gayle Mitchell is considered one of North America's leading experts on casino gaming and has made a career out of educating other gamblers. Here she explains the best and worst bets in the casino, the secrets of successful slots and video poker play, how to win at blackjack, her ten "Dos" of casino gambling, tips on casino poker, and much more. Her book is essential reading. $17.95 paperback

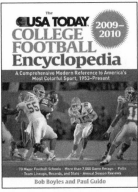

This is without question the most comprehensive resource on college football ever set to type. Here are 1,400 pages with recaps of 7,000 games, reviews of more than fifty-five seasons, complete season-by-season lineups and records of more than seventy major programs, personality profiles of some of the game's biggest stars and coaches, award winners, All-American teams, polls, NFL drafts, and more. $24.95 paperback

AVAILABLE WHEREVER BOOKS ARE SOLD
IN STORES AND ONLINE